KANG Woo-suk

Korean Film Directors

The Korean Film Directors series is one of Korean Film Council's projects to furnish an international audience with insight and analysis into the works of Korea's most representative film directors.

The series aims to expand upon the existing body of knowledge on Korean film, educate the general public of the history of Korean film and Korean film directors, and draw attention to the significance of works that represent Korean film. Critics who share their insight in the series are leaders in their respective specialties. Each volume includes critical commentary on films, an extensive interview with the director, and a comprehensive filmography for reference.

KANG Woo-suk

Written by OH Dong-jin
Translated by Colin A. Mouat

KANG Woo-suk

Written by OH Dong-jin

Korean Film Council
206-46 Cheongnyangni-dong, Dongdaemun-gu, Seoul 130-010, Korea
Phone (82-2) 9587-596
Fax (82-2) 9587-590
http://www.kofic.or.kr/english
email: pdh21@kofic.or.kr

Published by **Seoul Selection**
B1 Korean Publishers Association Bldg., 105-2 Sagan-dong, Jongno-gu, Seoul 110-190, Korea
Phone (82-2) 734-9567
Fax (82-2) 734-9562
http://www.seoulselection.com
email: pubco@seoulselection.com

ISBN: 978-89-91913-42-4 03680

Printed in the Republic of Korea

Contents

Preface

In Korean cinema, there are few figures as controversial as KANG Woo-suk. The controversy surrounding him has to do with the presence of many qualities outside of the aesthetic—commercial qualities—rather than purely aesthetic ones in his films. In the process, the fact that KANG Woo-suk is a veteran director of commercial film who has made 16 films in the 20 years from 1988 to 2008 has been frequently overlooked in Korea. Among the film directors of a similar generation to KANG, active in Korea since 1980, only BAE Chang-ho has made more than 16 films. Many Korean directors known widely overseas, for example LEE Chang-dong, HONG Sangsoo, PARK Chan-wook or KIM Jee-woon, have thus far been unable to reach even half that number.

It is surprising that KANG Woo-suk has not very often received proper attention in terms of the qualities of his films. This comes as a result of aspects of Korean cinema that have unconsciously undervalued the role of commercial film to such an extent. Thus, the reevaluation of KANG Woo-suk and his works provides an important starting point toward opening up a new view of Korean commercial film.

KANG's relatively 'unjust' treatment as a filmmaker thus far has been a result of a cinematic career treading a position at the farthest boundaries. He is a director, but he is also an investor and producer; he is an 'artisan' who makes films, but he has also been the merchant selling them. On one hand, he has succeeded in currying favor by protecting and supporting cinematic art, but on the other, he has also succeeded in generating a considerable number of critics by, for the sake of thoroughness, applying a cold business role for himself as well.

In the world of Korean film, KANG Woo-suk was once criticized for being a monopolist who owned production campany, film investment & distribution campany and theaters as well, but even then, there were very few people attacking him head on. Even the people criticizing him were awed to see him invest vast amounts of production costs in director IM Kwon-taek's *Chwihwaseon* and *Low Life* without hesitation, disregarding commercial profits. The people who envied him disparaged him even more as a director when they saw his outstanding knack for the business of film, but every time, he would silence his critics with massive hits such as *Silmido* and the *Public Enemy* series.

KANG may be scaling back to some extent recently, but it would be difficult to refute that, during the period from 2000 to 2005 when Korean film was solidifying its position in world cinema, it was the formation of such a solid base for the film industry at home that enabled directors such as IM Kwon-taek, LEE Chang-dong, HONG Sangsoo, KIM Ki-duk and PARK Chan-wook to win directors' prizes at major film festivals such as Cannes, Berlin, Venice and Karlovy Vary and enjoy a dazzling spotlight, and that KANG Woo-suk was central figure in forming that base.

KANG has consistently performed the background role of a man of power in Korean film for the last ten years. He has made only 16 films as a director since his debut in 1988, but for the more than ten years since 1997, he has been in charge of investment, planning or production for a full 120 films. It could be said that directors like IM Kwon-taek and LEE Chang-dong as well owe him a rather large debt, so great has his influence on Korean film been.

In spite of this, the name of KANG Woo-suk remains sequestered from the overseas film world. His films have thus far received little in the way of proper attention abroad. To some, he is known merely as a director specializing in Korean comedies. But his films have succeeded in capturing the rapidly changing Korean social and political situation of the last 20 years in a distinctive style, specifically a style of popular speech through satire and humor. Looking at his films in sequence, one can grasp the twists and turns of the history of Korean capitalism.

From time to time, KANG has made plain-speaking political films, demonstrating the breadth of his genre interest. These attempts have frequently failed, but when viewed in its totality, his success as the box office to date is close to the stuff of legend in Korean film.

To put it simply, KANG is the most successful figure in Korean film in terms of communication with the audience. Conversely, his films also provide an important standard in gauging how Korean film audiences have changed over the past 20 years and what the present level is for their attitudes and tastes toward film.

This book is a record of KANG's cinematic career over the past 20 years, and at the same time a document showing how Korean cinema possesses a fountain of diverse films and how considerable the potential of commercial film is.

July 2008

OH Dong-jin

On the Director

On the Director

Viewed simply from his filmography of 16 films, the course of KANG Woo-suk's works appears somewhat cautiously attuned to public sentiments. As is so often the case with directors of commercial film, from teen movies to romantic comedies, political films and social satirical dramas, it feels as through he has simply found a story conveniently suited to the circumstances of the time, cobbling something together and putting it out in theaters. But that is not enough to explain why KANG's films have almost every time been massive hits by Korean standards. His films have always grasped and reflected the desires of Korean audiences precisely. This is both an element in the success of nearly every one of KANG's films and the consistent 'something' possessed by his works. That 'something' is the plain-spoken social consciousness and social thematic awareness that KANG possesses.

What is interesting is how KANG's plain-spoken approach to social issues does not cause any particular conflict within the films. Thus, as commercial films, his works appear to fit into the lineage of realist film. Whether or not KANG himself has consciously realized it, he has effectively been making a sort of realist commercial film thus far.

KANG's films continuously set their footing firmly within commercialism and create a gaze that views society from that position. Interestingly enough, in spite of his being a director thoroughly aimed at commercial film, he consistently performs acts of political correctness. Thus, his films are frequently excessively direct and simple, textbook-like and moral. For this reason, they are perceived by some of the younger generation as old-fashioned.

The central theme for understanding KANG's films is the emotion of social rage felt by an individual possessing values of justice, where good ultimately triumphs over evil, toward a reality in which evil usually dominates good. Yet his commercial film strategy occasionally involves creating nasty and malicious characters, while intentionally removing the 'good guy' from his films. In this way, he pushes chaotic action and scattered gang fighting, but by the very end, what remains is the good: The values of good triumphing over evil. If the motto of Hollywood commercial film is "The hero never dies," the motto of KANG's films is "The good man never dies."

It is his most recent film, *Public Enemy Returns*, that most clearly shows this quality of KANG. The main character, GANG Cheol-jung, is a character from whom the image of the good detective is removed completely from the very beginning. GANG is portrayed as being only a shade more virtuous than the villain who is his counterpart. The director has long worked to strengthen the image of this character as noxious and dirty rather than good. But it is soon apparent toward whom this fiercely tenacious personality is directed. The viewers already recognize why his personality is so 'noxious.'

KANG Woo-suk is concerned about how easily his films could slip into a simple dualistic structure of good and evil. For this reason, the good characters in his films appear highly crazy and malicious on the outside. But to a certain point, this is merely for show. KANG's concept of good and evil is apparent, and his films are thus clear and concise. This is also the part that commercial film audiences are expecting: clearly resolving the problems of the world and bringing them concisely to a conclusion. From this, one can discern the reason for his films' continued

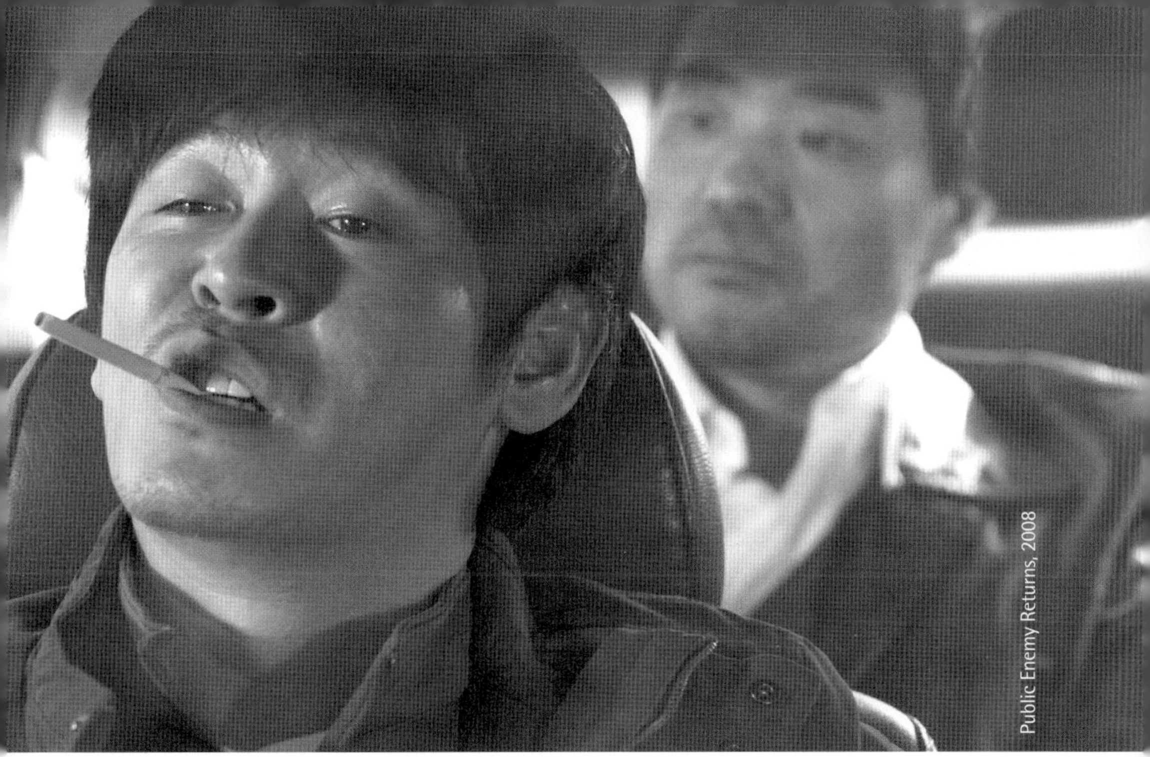

Public Enemy Returns, 2008

popular success in Korea.

The characters KANG portrays and the drama that accompanies them often travel the boundaries of hypocrisy and affected evil to a dangerous degree, but the themes that he presents are simple and transparent: truth and sincerity prevail. The plausible story, entertaining spectacle, laughter, humor and crude attitude toward the common good are added on top of this. KANG's films greatly boost the level of popular preferences in that they enable the viewer to see a great universe through a small telescope, to imagine a great universe through a small universe, to imagine it at least in a hopeful way.

Looking carefully at KANG's films, it can be seen that they have highly journalistic qualities. The themes he discusses are often stories that have become major social issues. The funny part is how often the social issues in his films have been portrayed either at almost exactly the same time as—or before—the real social issues have risen to the fore. This involves precisely grasping, in an animalistic and instinctual way, what will become a social issue in the future, and when viewed from this angle, KANG can be seen to have the necessary makings of a journalist as well as a director.

A good example of this is *Public Enemy Returns*, part of the aforementioned series. The main character, GANG Cheol-jung, grills meat at a Korean beef restaurant operated by mobsters and keeps yelling for someone to change the grill top. GANG begins picking a fight over various things with the mid-level boss who comes to restrain him, and eventually begins to ask whether the beef he's eating is really Korean beef. The boss says that their restaurant rigorously follows the practice of labeling the origin of its products, but GANG merely snorts. Grumbling, he asks where in Korean society someone can believe the country-of-origin labels on beef.

When the director decided to insert the beef story into the script of *Public Enemy Returns* as an episode along the way, it was during the planning stages of the film; beef had not yet had become a major social issue. But when *Public Enemy Returns* hit the theaters, daily candlelight protests were taking place in Korean society over the importation of American beef. Korean audiences felt a sense of catharsis at KANG's film because of precisely this prescient sense of his for the trends of the times. On their picket signs, Korean demonstrators used the expression "Public Enemies" to refer to the police and the government, and this shows how KANG's films were already something branded with the public.

1988~1992

One interesting thing is that it is possible to infer Korea's modern history, its last 20 years of social history, back from KANG's films. Every time he makes a film, he seeds it with the social issues of the time.

His 1988 debut, *Sweet Brides*, featured matinee idols at the peak of their popularity and was packaged plausibly as a romantic comedy, but the film in fact faithfully captures the social situation of the year in which it was released. The

Korean society of 20 years ago was at a time where an extreme gap between the rich cities and the poor farming villages was growing, a primary manifestation of the class polarization resulting from rapid industrialization. The 1980s' repressive CHUN Doo-hwan military dictatorship and the pseudo-democratic government that succeeded it concentrated on protecting things so that a specific minority could accumulate wealth through the sacrifice of the lower classes. *Sweet Brides* is a film that stressed how it cannot be in any way "sweet" for those with nothing, those who cannot study because they have nothing, and thus who cannot hold power in society, to get the girl (even one who is low-class enough to have an image close to that of a prostitute).

Sweet Brides is clearly a work that leans on the psychological legacy of director LEE Chang-ho's 1980 film *A Windy but Pleasant Day*. That film as well depicts the episodes encountered by three men (Deok-bae, Chun-sik and Gil-nam) who have come to Seoul from the country and work, respectively, as a staff member at a Chinese restaurant, an apprentice at a barbershop and a clerk at an inn (in Korea, such jobs are still categorized as low-class). Deok-bae feels passionate love for a married woman he meets delivering Chinese food, but it comes to nothing. The three of them get together one day and travel for an outing to the suburbs, deciding they need to recharge their lives, and end up meeting and hanging out with some female university students who have come to the same place. But the three men merely endure considerable teasing from the students, who intend only to toy with them as a joke. *A Windy but Pleasant Day* shows, with a comic yet melancholy touch, how empty and diabolical the proclaimed capitalist values of offering equal opportunities for social advancement to everyone are, and how genuine emotions get trampled and destroyed in the process.

If *A Windy but Pleasant Day* was the first work to announce, in a roundabout way, the dismal age of the 1980s in Korea, KANG's debut, *Sweet Brides* was a work that encapsulated how the 1980s were coming to an end in much the same way.

KANG mentions this in the following interview as well, but he does not hesitate to select LEE Chang-ho as his cinematic mentor. Frequently dragged to the theater by his film buff mother since his early childhood, KANG learned what he knows about life through the movies. As such, it is in some sense natural that he came to be aware of the absurdity of Korean society through the movies as well.

In the process, it was LEE Chang-ho's *A Windy but Pleasant Day* that played a decisive role in KANG Woo-suk's views on society, politics and life. He saw the film in his third year of high school, a year before he entered university. Essentially, he learned through that film how film can ensure an opportunity for social speech, and what aspects of society film can discuss.

KANG never worked on LEE Chang-ho's production team, nor did he apprentice under him. Viewed from the standards of Korean film, this is a bit out of the ordinary. Nevertheless, LEE Chang-ho and his film *A Windy but Pleasant Day* would be among the most important keys toward understanding KANG's films and his cinematic career. When KANG later made another major work, 1991's *Who Saw the Dragon's Claws?*, it was at the suggestion of LEE Chang-ho.

Who Saw the Dragon's Claws? was the film through which KANG proved to himself that it was possible to realize his interest in the orthodox political film cinematically. He has often bristled at being called a mere comedy director over the past 20 years. Each time, he has made heavily political films like *Silmido* and *Hanbando*, out of a desire to revive memories of his past with *Who Saw the Dragon's Claws?*.

As mentioned previously, KANG and his films often feel like journalistic records. KANG dropped out of college early and never experienced the university streets of the 1980s, boiling cauldrons of anti-government protest. Rather than seeking out practical wisdom in the lecture halls or books, or through direct experience by yelling slogans in the streets, he found it in the headlines of newspaper articles. For this reason, much of his cinematic material has come from the local news section rather than the political section, but during the early period of KANG's filmmaking career—the late 1980s to early 1990s—the political pages in Korean newspapers did not report facts as they actually occurred. What he considered social truth was more to be found on the local news pages than in the political section. The motif for *Sweet Brides* as well was found in the difficult

Sweet Brides, 1988

environment of the late 1980s, where young men in farming towns found it difficult to find wives in their regions, and the resulting cases of suicide.

For this reason, KANG's films, while having the basic structure of comedies, often mix in many depressing episodes, and thus come to have a heavily black comic quality.

KANG's first hit came with 1989's *Happiness Isn't Class Rankings, You Know*, which demonstrated how this relatively recent newcomer (who wasn't actually a newcomer—since beginning his work in film in 1984, KANG was aided by the connections of his action film star brother KANG Yong-seok and built an "inner circle" from early on, forming relatively tight connections with young directors and critics who dreamed of a new film movement) would soon become a top commercial director dominating Korean film. Though the film debuted on only two screens in Seoul, it eventually hit it big enough to pull in around 300,000 viewers before it left theaters. In an atmosphere of new growth of Korean film commercially, including the entrance into the Korean market of major Hollywood distributors like UIP, *Happiness Isn't Class Rankings, You Know* was treated as a mere independent picture, but with the pure popular appeal of film, it swept aside bigger films and put up an extraordinary fight at the box office. At that time, average yearly audience numbers in Korea stood at less than 20 million. Today, the total yearly audience attendance figures are at around 170 million. In view of this fact, a simple mathematical comparison shows that it was a film that generated huge box office for a work by a rookie director.

Happiness Isn't Class Rankings, You Know touched upon the issue of public education, one of the chronic ills facing Korean society. The landscape of a high school classroom, portrayed through the main characters of Bong-gu and Eun-ju, shows a microcosm of Korean capitalist society, with abnormal development and distorted growth repeated time and time again.

Dead last in his class, and a troublemaker to boot, Bong-gu has been regarded as a subject for segregation by Korean society from early on. He has a crush on Eun-ju, a top student who always fights for first or second place in class, but who is far from happy on the inside. For a school curriculum that is like a rite of passage to be passed through in order to advance one's status, the adolescent landscape of Bong-gu, Eun-ju and the friends surrounding them is heartbreaking and pitiful.

But KANG carefully hides the actually inevitably tragic story of these children behind the conventional expressive mechanisms of the teen movie. While feigning cheerfulness and lightness on the outside, the film consistently shows the innocent expressions of the children, ratcheting up the tension by hinting that the seeds of a darker story that shows through intermittently will ultimately explode later like a

Happiness Isn't Class Rankings, You Know, 1989

time bomb. Through a very conventional genre film, KANG denounces the irrationality hidden beneath the surface of Korean society. With a commercial film, he had succeeded at a realist's raising of issues.

In response to the popularity enjoyed by *Happiness Isn't Class Rankings, You Know*, some critics took pains to disparage it for being a youth film focusing on teenagers. But the level of popularity of the film was that explosive. If this was the case, it meant that the film had obtained a universal thematic awareness that transcended the adolescent segment. Indeed, *Happiness Isn't Class Rankings, You Know* was perceived by older audiences as indirectly reproaching the excessively class-based nature and irrational hierarchism of Korean society. The film forced audiences to reflect on a real situation where, in spite of the fact that happiness is not something material, like grades or possessions, but is something more qualitative, created through spiritual values, children were not being properly educated about this.

The film shows its genristic evolution in the climactic section. Yearning to break free from the yoke of tests and grades, Eun-ju ultimately cannot deal with the psychological pressures and chooses suicide. This tragic ending, a difficult choice for a teen film, argues that happiness is not about class rankings, but was ultimately judged to have succeeded in realistically portraying a tragic youth discouraged by the fact that happiness in Korean society is imposed by grades.

After the huge success of *Happiness Isn't Class Rankings, You Know*, KANG made two more teen films: 1991's *Teenage Love Song* and 1992's *I Only Want to Live to 20*. Compared to its predecessor, *Happiness Isn't Class Rankings, You Know*, *Teenage Love Song* went a step further in the direction of social issues.

The film actually only pretends to focus on youth issues, overlaying issues regarding the dismissal of teachers from the Korean Teachers' and Education Workers' Union, who had become the target of conservatives in Korean society at the time. A number of vested interests in Korea had been accumulating massive untaxed riches through schools and religious foundations, for a long time sowing the seeds of social discord. Some teachers with a progressive consciousness created labor unions within the schools to oppose this, and the conservatives of Korean society mobilized existing systems and laws to repress them as impure elements implanting socialist ideas in the students. In the film, KANG seems to lump together schools and religion as objects of criticism, and includes a scene where, as the children head to school, their parents make a scene blocking off two dismissed teachers struggling to return to work. The parents quibble about how the children cannot be sacrificed because of the teachers, and the principal, as a principal would, ideologically represses the central character of Jecheol by saying that teachers can't properly hold preparation classes for the university entrance exam when they're going on only about what is true education and how students should be treated as a whole individual. Meanwhile, Jun-seok is enough of a problem child to be suspended four times, and in the scene that shows why he has come to have such a twisted psyche, he goes home and we see the shoes of the church members that always fill his doorway. Instead of her son's education, his mother is only interested in her own religious salvation, but she is failing to save herself, her child or her home.

The film's central character, Jun-seok, comes to his senses only when the teacher who was always the target of his acts of rebellion comes to seem like something other than a teacher. It is because of Je-cheol, who has taken over Jun-seok's homeroom class. But when Je-cheol's co-worker is fired for being affiliated with the teacher's union, his troubles begin to mount. Je-cheol and Jun-seok, their classmate Chae-ok (Je-cheol's younger sister, whom Jun-seok likes), and the bookish youth Hyeong-su (who forms a triangle with Jun-seok and Chae-ok) come to find themselves heading toward catastrophe as tensions deepen more and more between the divided school and teachers' union members.

An interesting part of *Teenage Love Song* is how it shows signs of the distinctive action scenes and minor characters that would appear in KANG's later films. The opening scene, where Je-cheol is walking along the street at night and is lynched by Jun-seok's gang, and the amateur gangster behavior shown by Jun-seok's group are interesting as early forms of the KANG Woo-suk villain characters who would appear later in *Two Cops* and the *Public Enemy* series.

1992's *I Only Want to Live to 20* is not a film with any especially notable qualities compared to the two teen social pieces that had preceded it. The film was based on the personal experience of KIM Chang-wan, the once-famous singer who had been the music director for *Happiness Isn't Class Rankings, You Know*. It tells the story of a girl who has contracted bone marrow cancer and is living on borrowed time. Perhaps KANG had become somewhat confident in his ability to capture the emotions of young audiences, as the film is relatively weak in dramatic tension compared to the two previous films. The director had taken a step back from his previous open criticism of the dark aspects of Korean society and taken as his material a heartwarming story of virtuous acts. Among KANG's early works, the film belongs to the category of human drama. The film failed to attract attention from a critical perspective, and inevitably remained at a basic level in terms of box office as well.

KANG's cinematic ambitions were revealed the previous year, with *Who Saw the Dragon's Claws?* which came out the same year as *Teenage Love Song*. This film seems to stand out the most among KANG's early works, but is pointed to, paradoxically, as the most typical of the director. In this early work, KANG commands the most direct political terminology, as much as with later works such as *Silmido* and *Hanbando*.

In order to understand *Who Saw the Dragon's Claws?*, one needs to trace the complex course of modern Korean political history. In 1987, presidential candidate ROH Tae-woo, a member of the ruling party that had broken down in the face of the citizens' "people power" and accepted the procedures of representative democracy, was a successor of the military dictatorship, but was elected after playing the spoiler in the division between the opposing party representatives, KIM Dae-jung and KIM Young-sam. However, in the following National Assembly elections, the Korean people voted for large opposition representation and small ruling party representation, curbing the government's power, and the ROH administration, feeling threatened by this, brought in former presidential candidate KIM Young-sam, who had been a powerful force in the opposition until then, and the conservative party candidate KIM Jong-pil, producing a coalition party from the three and creating a political situation where the ruling party representation

Who Saw the Dragon's Claws?, 1991

was comparatively greater. This political incident was called the three-party merger—or three-party collusion—and led to the regression of Korean politics.

Who Saw the Dragon's Claws? deals with the presidential election, telling the story of the political collusion of the conservative ruling party, which is attempting to reach secret deals, and a leader in the opposition party. The film begins with the brutal lynching death of a presidential candidate, a former martial law administrator and member of a hard-line conservative faction. He is discovered drowned in a reservoir, and theories circulate about whether his death was a suicide or murder; meanwhile, a famous television anchor who witnessed the incident decides to keep quiet about it for the sake of a powerful opposition candidate with whom she has entered an illicit relationship. But with the advice and encouragement of an older reporter at the broadcasting company, she eventually reveals the truth. In the process, a newspaper reporter investigating the incident with them is kidnapped by organization members and tortured.

The film was made in 1991, but it focuses on revealing a dark shadow of political oppression that is still hanging over Korean society today. A media still oppressed with acts of censorship, opposition party leaders busily hiding their scandals while trumpeting justice and righteousness, political terrorism taking place between ruling conservative factions—*Who Saw the Dragon's Claws?* attempts to depict the oppressive Korean political situation faithfully.

The film was KANG's first attempt at a political thriller. Its basic political thriller structure focuses on the question of who killed the Assemblyman. Did the orders for the murder come from the ruling party? To what extent did the opposition candidate participate in the conspiracy? Will the reporter protagonist and the people around her show the courage to dig up the truth, or will they bow to political intimidation? The film works to provide strands of tension until the last.

What is interesting is how the film creates many complex characters. The newspaper reporter who exposes the truth first breaks under torture, intimidation and appeasement, confessing that the report was a fabrication, and another colleague, who has long worked as a pawn of the government media, plans a double-cross so that the main character can get to the truth of the incident. The many complex characters built up around the main character play a large part in enriching the overall dramatic structure, and the same technique worked to strengthen cinematic interest when used extensively by KANG in the *Two Cops* and *Public Enemy* series.

At the time of its release, *Who Saw the Dragon's Claws?* was highly underrated, but among KANG's early films, it is worthy of selection along with *Happiness Isn't Class Rankings, You Know* as a major work. The film is impeccable in its polish as well, with its overall story structure, gradually heightening tension and realism in recreating the actual political reality. However, it appears that the reason for the film's inability to gather audience interest was an acknowledgement that the film's content was too closely connected with reality. It is not easy for a film to outdo a political reality with various dramatic storylines of its own. In Korean society it is frequently the case that the reality is more cinematic. In this regard, it seems that films like *Who Saw the Dragon's Claws?* or the later *Hanbando*, political films in which KANG directly employed his discourse, were limited from the beginning in terms of audience response. But through this film, he proved that he was a craftsman capable of making films with diverse subject matter and showed that Korean film could achieve considerable results in the political thriller genre as well.

If *Who Saw the Dragon's Claws?* was the most ambitious of KANG's early works, then *I Stand Up Every Day*, made a year earlier, belongs among his most novel. Most of all, it is his funniest film, and it is worthy of note for comprehensively laying out examples of socially satirical grammar using the character comedy shown consistently in his later works.

I Stand Up Every Day grabs attention from its opening scene. Wearing a wide trench coat, the protagonist makes faces and enters a bank just before closing. Looking around to see if anyone notices, he waits until the moment the bank's shutter comes down and then takes out a military rifle from within his coat and takes over the scene. After rounding up the people with seasoned skill and filling a bag with money, he steps out of the bank to find himself—oops—surrounded by police.

In this scene, reminiscent of Al Pacino's bank robbery scene in *Dog Day Afternoon*, the audience expects the protagonist to go back into the bank and take hostages, but suddenly the man starts firing his gun recklessly at the police instead. He ends up falling under the storm of gunfire of the police, and at this point the film cuts to a gunfight scene from John Woo's *The Killer* and shows the protagonist sleeping in the theater and starting to scream and talk in his sleep as he is shot in his dream. It turns out that the bank robbery scene that came before was all this man's dream, and from the beginning the film shows in a single stroke that the protagonist is currently living a sad and pathetic existence.

Having faithfully brought the audience in from the introduction, the film goes on to make them laugh with the ironic story of the man's situation. The protagonist, Baek-su (in Korean, this is also a noun that refers to an unemployed person who plays around all the time) has barely graduated from a Seoul university thanks to tuition paid by his country farmer parents with money they did or did not have (even selling their cow, which farmers view as something as important as their children), but after two years he still has not found a job. He cooks for himself in a small room in an old-fashioned Korean-style house and goes around from place to place looking for work, but nothing goes right for him. With his pockets always empty, he trembles with fear even when eating a 2,000 won bowl of soup, and, as is always the case with people when they have no money, the portions are never big enough. One day, he is eating soup at the restaurant and succeeds in sneaking some of the rice soup that another customer has left at the next table, intending to give it to someone. Satisfied and digging in to his heart's content, Baek-su has eaten almost all of it when he is shocked to see that the person who bought the food is giving it to his dog.

Baek-su cannot do anything with Eun-sil, the woman he has a crush on. An accountant at a neighborhood supermarket, she is pestered by the uneducated and boorish owner, but Baek-su is always bested by the man. While imbuing the owner's character with comic elements, KANG does not hesitate to shed a cynical gaze on him. The swaggering owner takes the employees of his supermarket to a Chinese restaurant and has a company dinner, going on about how they should eat whatever they want. But he himself orders a cheap bowl of noodles with black bean sauce. The employees, with sour expressions on their faces, have no choice but to order the same thing.

Seeing Baek-su running around—sometimes because of Eun-sil, sometimes because of the villainous supermarket owner, sometimes because of the lustful advances of a strange woman he happens to meet—the audience bursts into laughter, but the continuing drama makes them realize that the laughter is not real laughter at all, and that they actually want to cry.

In this film, KANG seems to pin the people down mercilessly, showing how sharply edged his social satire is. Scenes such as the one where the supermarket owner makes a report to the police in order to tear Baek-su away from Eun-sil allude to how the Korean society of the early 1990s was still a closed society, a tightly blocked society. When the owner is unable to prove to the police that Baek-su is an unsavory element, a former student activist, he hurls the telephone and launches into right-wing polemic, going on about how the anti-Communist spirit has faded and how they need to keep these people back.

At his wits' end, Baek-su tries to get a job at a production factory, a place where university graduates rarely go. At first, the human resources official politely refuses him, and then after Baek-su closes the door and leaves, he begins yelling, "Did you think you were going to fool me again? They need to beat down all these college students coming to stir things up in the factories."

The intermittently concealed social codes show how KANG has no shortage of things to say about the Korean society of the late 1980s and early 1990s through his film. It starts out as a comedy, but by the time that Eun-sil is just on the verge of being raped, audience laughter has been silenced. The film criticizes the rapid change of affairs in Korean society toward a petty capitalism that seeks to rape "Eun-sil/the people", since she has no money and it seems like money can buy anything. The society that seemed to say that happiness is about class ranking, that you have to graduate from university, and that everything will be guaranteed if you just graduate from a university, now merely stands by irresponsibly after generating countless "slackers" like Baek-su. In such a thoroughly hierarchized society, people like the protagonist Baek-su struggle to get up every day, as the film's title states, but the film sighs that this may be a vain dream. The fact that the original title of *I Stand Up Every Day* was *Baegilmong (Daydream)* underscores this.

In the string of early works that went from his debut *Sweet Brides*, with its influence from LEE Chang-ho's *A Windy but Pleasant Day*, through *Happiness Isn't Class Rankings, You Know* and on to *I Stand Up Every Day* and *Who Saw the Dragon's Claws?*, KANG Woo-suk focused on proving that he was someone who could make films with a strong social and political character. If, out of these works, *I Stand Up Every Day* and *Who Saw the Dragon's Claws?* had been the biggest box office successes, KANG might well be in a quite different trajectory today. But with *Happiness Isn't Class Rankings, You Know* becoming his biggest work at the time, KANG began to focus on softer films as he entered the second stage of his directorial activity. The first work of this second period was *Mister Mama*, a film that brought in a wave of screwball comedies in Korea.

1992~1998

Released in 1992, the same year as *I Only Want to Live to 20, Mister Mama* is the film that deviates the most from the trajectory of KANG's filmography. This film did succeed admirably in putting KANG's name once again onto the list of successful commercial directors, but one hesitates to call it a "KANG Woo-suk movie". Generally, it is placed boldly among KANG's major works, but a glance at his previous works shows that it is this film that hits the most discordant notes. It is difficult to find any of the heated anger toward the world shown in previous films like *I Stand Up Every Day*. Furthermore, the minor laughs and mood-lightening humor that could be called KANG's forte are scarcely to be found.

If one looks back at 1992, it seems like a period of searching for KANG Woo-suk. In this regard, it is difficult to argue that *I Only Want to Live to 20* as well was a tautological piece in which KANG seemed to copy his own two previous teen films.

Mister Mama functioned as a central point in moving KANG more surely toward the commercial film sphere. The film is so thoroughly planned out that it is difficult to view as a critical text. Indeed, *Mister Mama* is judged to have served as a kind of signal announcing the introduction of a producer system in modern Korean film history. Before then, the Korean film industry was operating under a somewhat pre-modern system, without necessary advancements and specialization having been realized. In many cases, production, direction and marketing tasks were not distinguished from one another. It's a story at a different level from independent films made under a kind of one-man production system.

It would not be an overstatement to say that the only work KANG Woo-suk did for *Mister Mama* was the direction. The production was handled by SHIN Cheol (who would later produce JANG Sun-woo's *Lies* and KWAK Jae-yong's *My Sassy Girl*) and YOO In-taek (who would later produce many films, including PARK Kwang-su's *A Single Spark* and KIM Ji-hun's *May 18*); the production head was CHA Seung-jae (who would later produce many films, including BONG Joon-ho's *Memories of Murder*); and the script was by KIM Hyeong-jun (who would later work on *Silmido*).

Mister Mama, 1992

These individuals all used the success of *Mister Mama* to establish their own film companies and begin production work, ushering in Korean film's "age of the producer" in earnest. It was as though an era of planned films was beginning for the first time in Korean film, and this would soon come to mean the creation of a surer foundation for the commercial film world. KANG Woo-suk as well used this work as a foothold for establishing "KANG Woo-suk Productions" and began to dive into the market more actively.

Insofar as it was a film in which the division of labor was accomplished systematically in a way rare for Korean film at the time, KANG was able to concentrate his energies only on directing. But this can also be interpreted as meaning that the margin for the director to intervene in the film was narrow.

That is really the sense one gets upon viewing the film. The protagonist Hyeong-jun (one can see how the film is flavored with the autobiographical story of the screenwriter, KIM Hyeong-jun), an employee at a video production and distribution company, drinks every night and comes home late. One day his wife abruptly leaves home, leaving behind their child, who is not yet one year old. Hyeong-jun is a patriarchal male who cannot believe that his wife has left, but he is forced into child-rearing operations for the first time in his life. Suddenly a single father, he takes the child to his company and is frantic trying to take care of the baby, having clashes in particular with his co-worker Yeong-ju. Yeong-ju fancies herself a confident modern woman, and she is at first unable to accept Hyeong-jun's situation, but gradually she grows closer to him and the two end up getting married.

A typical episodic drama, the film flavors each section with comedy bordering on slapstick. The unsightly image of Hyeong-jun acting crazy trying to raise his child is played for laughs, and KANG supplies the individual scenes written in the script without expression. There are few traces of particular concern about the work to be found. It merely reflects, with a light touch, how the Korean society of the time was at a stage where new women were starting to appear, looking for new role models in the home; where the woman's search for her identity was being actively discussed; and where the long-maintained Confucian feudalism and patriarchal order in Korean society was disintegrating. And this point is judged to have perhaps appealed to women viewers in their early 20s, who were on the rise as a major audience in theaters, thus contributing to the great success of the film at the box office.

Following the two 1992 films, KANG went through a period of relative inactivity after running breathlessly for four years straight since his debut. Quickly on his way to the top, KANG suddenly found himself hesitant about where to go next in a changing era for film and making films in a conventional way. It was inevitable that the two films would have a somewhat regressive feel.

But the director immediately succeeded at finding his way again, as he managed to make the most important film of his cinematic career. That film was *Two Cops*.

Two Cops left a significant mark both in terms of KANG Woo-suk's overall filmography and Korean film as a whole. Most notably, it announced the arrival of a properly finished socially satirical drama for the first time in post-1970s Korean film.

It was possible because freedom of creative expression, at least formally, had broken free from the taboos that had hung over it in Korean society before then. Korean governmental authorities may have overcome their allergic reaction to films dealing with political incidents (this was the background in which films like *Who Saw the Dragon's Claws?* had been made), but at the time there were still groups that were not to be touched within the consciousness of the Korean ruling class. At the top of this list were the military, the police, the prosecutor's office and public officials. *Two Cops* tittered at the core of a Korean society still dominated by a conservative social consciousness and let fly with open derision. This cynicism of KANG's toward Korean society was suddenly met with an enthusiastic welcome from audiences.

But the true mission of *Two Cops* is not only in indicting the hypocrisy and false villainy of conservatives in a Korea trapped within thick walls. The film had a somewhat broader meaning in possessing a universal sentiment that went beyond that. *Two Cops* is a film that recommends relaxing somber attitudes toward the old generation and new generation, old age and newness, the disappearing and the newly appearing, a closed society and opening society, and discussing a solution with a lighter atmosphere. It was a time in which rapid deconstructions were taking place everywhere throughout Korean society. *Two Cops* stood at the boundary of what was passing by and what was newly arriving and encouraged reconciliation between the two.

The protagonists of *Two Cops* are police detectives, one an old veteran and one a rookie. The mainstay of the film is frantic confrontation created between the two. The veteran Detective JO has considerable authority and is used to throwing his weight around in his jurisdiction. His daily business is limited to shaking down pocket change, from roadside stands to upstanding entertainment spots. His world view is that the world isn't going to change no matter what he himself does, and tends further toward the idea that the world never changes at all; idealism is just idealism, and the more you try to apply those ideals, the more things in the world will end up screwed up. JO's philosophy of life may seem absurd and unfair, but it does indeed have practical aspects for living. Meanwhile, the rookie Detective GANG, just placed after graduating from the police college, has a view that is 180 degrees opposite from JO's: he believes that you can make all of the corruption and impropriety of the world disappear by following your principles to the end.

The episodes resulting from their quarreling provide belly laughs for the viewer. Detective JO drags Detective GANG from place to place in order to tell him, "No matter how high-mindedly you cling to your ideals, what is someone like you going to do when you face the real situation up close?" The scene of the two of them conducting a visual inspection of a murder scene has become one of the film's legendary moments. JO begins poking carelessly at a body left in the trunk of a car, and GANG, unable to bear the stench, begins to throw up his guts. Seeing Detective GANG, who until that point had been strict and single-minded, collapsing in an instant with a comical expression on his face, the audience can sense that the story is not going to go the way he expects it to.

Another funny scene involves the questioning of a low-level gangster. The gangster, who has been in and out of police stations repeatedly and has racked up a considerable list of priors, finds Detective GANG amusing. When the rules of interrogation don't go over one bit, Detective JO sends GANG out and begins

Two Cops, 1993

hurting himself in front of the criminal, which leads him to confess to the crime.

Two Cops shows that this is a method that likely won't go over with a new age and a new generation, but that the world will not work properly if we completely ignore the things of the past. And if the things of the past stay only in the past, they just become an impediment to the development of the times. For this reason, the deeper we get into the later part of the film, the more episodes there are where the two detectives join forces. *Two Cops* demonstrates that changes in the times must be created by old but wise knowledge and immature but new thinking.

The fact that KANG Woo-suk himself is a middle generation film director wedged between conservatism and progressivism, between the old and the new, and between stasis and change is interpreted as an element that led him to make this film with himself embodied in it. The director was at a time when he had entered Korean film as a youngster in the previous generation, learned his craft, and was working with the status of elder brother to the new generation. For KANG, the characters of Detectives JO and GANG in *Two Cops* also signified the two generations of Korean film.

Two Cops also featured the overall polished cinematic technique that the director would adopt in his later work. With the experience he gleaned from this film—a well-constructed narrative, frame construction, action scene filming (for example, in mob scenes) and the development of diverse supporting characters to support the leads—KANG created a manual of techniques for his later films. Through *Two Cops*, he also extended his sense of humor greatly. It was at this point that people began to say of him, "He's gotten more humor."

In short, the film satisfies those who view it with a light sense of rhythm. For them, the rhythm of the overall construction and the rhythm of individual sequences seem to combine organically, creating a pleasant spectacle where all the overall elements come together just right. For example, the actions of Detective JO as he enters his home, identified only as an address so that he can disguise himself as poor, is hilarious because of its rhythm. He opens up an old-fashioned telephone set and takes out a modern wireless model, and from next to his cramped bed he pulls out expensive liquor that no common person could ever afford. KANG shoots the scene in one continuous take, and the effect is reminiscent of Gene Kelly doing his tap dance in the rain in *Singin' in the Rain.*

The huge success of *Two Cops* led to predictions that a sequel was soon to follow. Indeed, 1996 would see the release of *Two Cops*, which centers on the character of Detective GANG and tells the story of two new detectives. This sequel clearly repeats the story of the previous installment, but some cleverness can be spied in how it makes the character of Detective GANG like Detective JO. In the second film, GANG has turned into a figure who takes after Detective JO from the first film like a carbon copy, and the newly deployed Detective LEE resembles the GANG from the first film. It has the same conception as and similar episodes to the first film, but the strength of the comedy has been raised, doubling the laughs.

In total, three episodes would be made in the series, though direction for the third installment was handled by KIM Sang-jin, who had been KANG's assistant director, while KANG handled production duties. Another mega-hit among KANG's films at the time was *Killing My Wife.* Released in 1994, between the first and second *Two Cops* films, it showed that KANG's comedy was forming a school of its own. Through this film, he began to be perceived among audiences as a specialist in comedy, and that misunderstanding continues to this day.

Killing My Wife, to put it simply, overturns all of the conventional ideas of Korean society. This is especially true with regard to the story, which deals with a man hiring a hit man to kill his wife. The gist of the film is an exhortation to go beyond disintegrating and into outright destroying the values of the home—perceived in Korean society as the final stronghold that must be held supreme—through the murder of the wife. This is essentially a fresh political declaration that Korean society has entered a time where the wife can now be the target of a murder. But the truly subversive sense of the film is in how it avoids making this into a passionate murder piece or a mystery thriller with a bizarre atmosphere, but instead turns it into a comedy from beginning to end, with riotous laughter generated from the ironic clash of situations.

Bong-su and So-yeong loved each other to death when they got married, but now they bicker constantly over everything. Bong-su feels humbled by his wife, who outdoes him at home and in her work. The complex he gets from her eventually develops into a desire to see her dead. But the hit man he hires, for all of the devious means he employs, always ends up suffering somehow at the hands of So-yeong. What is funny in the film is how So-yeong, who doesn't even know that she is a target, always ends up escaping the killer's threat through sheer coincidence. The killer, in a manner scarcely befitting a hit man, is scared out of his wits trying to save his own skin.

Killing My Wife gives the impression of KANG Woo-suk following through on areas where he felt bad about not being able to reveal his own thoughts in *Mister Mama*. While the film acknowledges that the role of women in Korean society has expanded to such an extent that they cannot be killed even if one tries, it says that we should accept this pleasantly.

The film also showed how KANG's comedy is based thoroughly in characters. He showed the trademark KANG Woo-suk character comedy developing into finished form from *Two Cops*.

What pulls the movie along is a series of ironic situations employed in diverse ways, but ahead of all of these situations, it is the characters of the husband and the hit man created by actors PARK Joong-hoon and CHOI Jong-won that create explosive laughter all by themselves. It was with the success of these two films, *Two Cops* and *Killing My Wife* that KANG Woo-suk began focusing on the creation of characters rather than story or images.

Bedroom and Courtroom is considered the most unexpected work of this period. It is difficult to view it as a continuation from *Two Cops* and *Killing My Wife*. KANG had, for the few years before then, been showing behavior that went outside of the scope of the works he had made. This may perhaps be seen as resulting from a desire to make diverse genre films and a habit of trying to show that he was a director who could make them well enough. *Bedroom and Courtroom* was made in an attempt to create a kind of courtroom drama that he had never attempted before.

In this film, KANG attempts to synthesize and employ all of his strengths. Most of all, he pulls social issues deeply into the film once again. As ever, he finds a

Bedroom and Courtroom, 1998

new class of the socially disadvantaged and takes their side.

The film tells the story of a woman who files a lawsuit on behalf of her husband, who is faced with the loss of his job despite years of service. But the item she selects for her lawsuit is not anything like an application for an injunction on the suspension. She says that, since her husband had been forced to neglect his 'service' to her as a husband because of his service to company, she had been forced to live as a neglected wife, and that the company therefore owes her damages for that.

In this film, a unique lawsuit (at least in Korean society) is shown taking place in court. In the process, the cast of characters is doubled and overlaid, with on one hand the "widow" and her husband and on the other the plaintiffs' attorney MYEONG Seong-gi and the defendants' attorney LEE Gi-ja. The two attorneys are husband and wife.

The film's angle of opposition is basically divided into the plaintiffs' and defendants' side, as represented by MYEONG and LEE respectively, but their relationship of contrast ends up more complexly intertwined in that they stand for problems of masculinism and feminism in Korea. Thus, relationships of both antagonism and camaraderie are formed within the story between LEE and the neglected wife protagonist, and between MYEONG and the husband. Underlying this are the exploitative hiring practices of a Korean company, identified as a conglomerate, and the image of hypocritical intellectual groups selling their souls on behalf of capital, forming various layers of episodes in the story.

Bedroom and Courtroom showed that KANG's line of sight on Korean society was shifting from political aspects to economic aspects. This, in turn, showed that

Korean society, while becoming more democratic politically, was faced with a situation of deepening subordination to capital and oppression by it. It was this aspect that KANG regarded as his new cinematic theme.

In this film, KANG focuses on untangling all of the know-how he had accumulated up until that point. He links comic situations through each character, creating another character comedy, while at the same time presenting another scathing social satire on the organizations of authority in Korean society, as he had done in *Who Saw the Dragon's Claws?* and *Two Cops*. This time, the satire is aimed at the courts and conglomerates.

Bedroom and Courtroom originally took its name from a play, which KANG adapted into a script and filmed. Its box office fell short of expectations. Because of its dismal box office, KANG had time to spend three years under the radar, and he spent this time devoting himself to planning and producing works for other directors rather than filming them himself. Around this time, in 1997, he also expanded his production company, KANG Woo-suk Productions, into the investment and distribution company Cinema Service. Through this gap of three years, KANG came to possess the name and authority of a cinematic entrepreneur, and a number of the some 120 films he has produced were made during this time.

2001~2008

After three years without directing any new films, KANG released *Public Enemy*, which was not originally expected to see as great a success financially as it did. KANG had simply needed a comeback piece, but the film's results went beyond expectations.

With *Public Enemy*, it is impossible to gauge what image KANG is going to present in his comeback simply by the first scene. GANG Cheol-jung and his older partner, Detective SONG Haeng-gi, have extorted money from a drug dealer during a drug investigation and are being pursued by internal affairs. The two of them park in a secluded spot on the beach near Incheon and discuss the situation.

With his disheveled appearance and disgusted expression, worn to the bone by life, GANG is made to seem closer to a criminal than a detective. From this first scene, it is clear that GANG is far from a righteous character.

The shock in this scene comes when GANG steps out of the car for a moment: feeling that he is at the end of his rope, SONG puts a gun to his head and, without a moment's hesitation, pulls the trigger. The stunned GANG gets back in the car and, rather than mourning the death of his colleague, he bellows and curses about how the older man has forced all the responsibility on him and taken the easy way out.

By choosing this noirish opening, KANG Woo-suk displays the resources to make the viewer attach in an instant to the character of GANG Cheol-jung, the director's alter ego in his new film: a man driven into this and that situation at the end of his rope. As he makes the absurd reality faced by GANG Cheol-jung come up against the absurd reality of the world surrounding him, the director begins to create a paradox of bitter laughter. An odd situation-driven drama follows, and inside of it, the director has characters already constructed with peculiar personalities romp freely. It is the moment at which a bitter human story unfolds, where a man cannot overcome evil in a world where evil dominates without becoming a beast himself.

In *Public Enemy*, KANG Woo-suk shows that his comedy is not ordinary comedy. At a time where the main trend in Korean film was romantic comedy, the director dismissed that as child's play and put forward a comedy with a more direct and powerful feeling. Grafting together comedy and a grisly murder story, he avoids clashes between the two while following through consistently on the basis of the comedy that is his strength, proving that he had evolved in terms of genre despite the passage of three years.

The story of *Public Enemy* has Detective GANG, restored to the force after a long series of events, getting involved in the investigation of the brutal murder of an old married couple. There is a funny moment when GANG, with his animalistically developed instinct and intuition, discovers the culprit. Instead of filming such an incident with a dazzling story structure and respectable

Public Enemy, 2008

atmosphere, KANG carries it out by having GANG taking a shit in the rain while on stakeout after eating bad food. Crouching in the rain and groaning, just as in his own chaotic situation, GANG slips on his own shit and stains his clothes. As he asks for help from the killer, JO Gyu-hwan, who happens to be passing by wearing a rain slicker, he is wounded by the man's knife. GANG connects this incident, which takes place in the course of an entirely different investigation, with the murder of the old couple, and with the scar of JO's knife attack still on his face, he sets out on a tenacious pursuit of the killer. The killer he happened to come across while taking a shit. Is GANG just a lucky guy? Is the killer just an unlucky guy? The absurdity created by this unusual story generates snickers from start to finish.

Returning to directing after three years, KANG Woo-suk demonstrates a knack for further strengthening his trademark character comedy. Besides the central character of GANG Cheol-jung, he includes various characters around him, confidently showing that he can generate a great deal of laughter just through the characters even before the events of the story begin.

The situation created by the head of the investigation in order to maintain the arraignment of the third-rate gangster GANG has arrested shows that the comedy can get real laughs just when it portrays something that goes a step beyond reality. Attempting to pin the crime on the gangster, a professional thief, the chief says that the weapon used was a flat-head screwdriver, and then erupts into a rage. He rummages noisily through the cabinet and finds a Philips head screwdriver, and then insists to the criminal that the screwdriver used was a Philips head, not a flat-head screwdriver. Thinking that it would be better to go up for a relatively weak robbery incident rather than take a harsher sentence for assault, the gangster is at a loss as to what to do, and the look on his face shows what the essence of character comedy is. Ironic situations where we don't know what to do are already part of our own daily lives. The viewers applaud and cheer GANG and the other investigators, in spite of the fact that they are clearly breaking and evading the law. In a word rife with extreme crimes and offenses, their deviations are accepted instead as realistic and practical.

The character of Yong-man, a knife-wielding thug always suspected by the police, performs a very important role in this film. The efficient harmonizing of a diverse cast of characters besides the lead character of GANG Cheol-jung heightens the humor of the situation. The film becomes more three-dimensional and complex because of such characters. The comedy typically generates laughs by continuously sticking together paradoxes and ironic situations, but *Public Enemy*'s characters create a humorous atmosphere at an explosive speed, so that it is impossible to keep up with where the situation is going. The fact that *Public Enemy* succeeded mightily at the box office in spite of certain weaknesses in the dramatic elements of the story owes itself to this.

The most controversial element in *Public Enemy* is JO Gyu-hwan, the extraordinary serial killer whom GANG is chasing. This man comes to realize the diabolical nature hidden within himself when he brutally slays his parents after they declare that they are going to bequeath their estate to a public welfare organization. JO murders a taxi driver for disrupting his driving, and then follows another man who spilled food on his clothes at a buffet and kills him indiscriminately as well. A man with two faces—a successful fund manager—JO Gyu-hwan murders without a shred of remorse or hesitation, with a satisfied smile on his face.

In order to show what a hypocritical and dangerous character he is, KANG shows a scene of him showering. Using the stream of water to masturbate, JO Gyu-hwan utters perverse curses, and by having this scene come relatively early on in the film, KANG uses it as a device to explain how abnormal the character is.

In spite of this, the character of JO Gyu-hwan was criticized by some for being excessively one-note in comparison with many of the other characters in the film. It is not explained convincingly why he is such a brutal character or how he became that way. But, oddly enough, random murders by psychopaths started to appear as a new trend of crime in Korean society after the release of *Public Enemy*. Director NA Hong-jin's *The Chaser*, which has recently generated major discussion and received plaudits from critics at the Cannes Film Festival, is another film that portrays an oddball serial killer embarking on a series of bizarre murders. With this being the case, the simply portrayed serial killer character in *Public Enemy* has sufficient grounds for vindication in that it sensed a bizarre current in Korean society before the fact. The director appears to have judged it better to raise the public's anger, if even for reasons as opaque as the character of the public enemy himself.

Such a choice by the director may have been accepted unquestioningly by the public, but not by critics. As if acknowledging this criticism, KANG made the character of the killer in the series' third installment, *Public Enemy Returns*, as subtle and complex as that of GANG Cheol-jung.

The public may not have known this, but *Public Enemy* bears the same title as a monumental gangster film made in 1931 starring James Cagney. Cagney's *Public Enemy* also told the story of a character considered shocking at the time, that of a gangster without a shred of remorse or conscience, expressing the extreme diabolical nature that a human can easily develop in capitalist society. The reason that this film is considered a legendary work is not the violence shown by the gangster in the film, but the cruelty within the character, with any hint of emotion absent.

Considered KANG's two major works, *Public Enemy* and *Two Cops* may have shrewdly borrowed their titles from an old Hollywood film and a European film with similar subject matter, but they are characterized by a way of Koreanizing the material or creating something completely new so that there is no sense of imitation. *Two Cops* recreated the 1984 French film *Les Ripoux (My New Partner)*, starring Philippe Noiret, as a Korean-style comedy, and *Public*

Enemy was transformed into a comedy that even those familiar with the James Cagney film could not have foreseen. Naturally, the films have completely different content as well. In the case of *Two Cops*, only the set-up of the juxtaposition of a veteran detective and a rookie is the same; the content and degree of the social satire are totally different.

Public Enemy was completed in 2001 and premiered in January 2002. The film drew more than 3 million viewers nationwide and demonstrated that KANG Woo-suk had not lost anything as a director of hit films. He went on to be recognized as a model director of Korean commercial film, and his legendary box office success showed that he was still invincible.

But KANG's commercial might really showed through with *Silmido*, the military action film that he began planning immediately after *Public Enemy* and released in 2003. The film accomplished the extraordinarily rare (in Korea) feat of drawing 10 million viewers to the theaters. It was a true blockbuster, earning 70 billion won in theater admissions alone.

Silmido dealt with material that had been considered taboo in Korea. The small island of Silmido, located in the ocean off the shore of Incheon, was the site of a hair-raising political/military plot in the late 1960s.

In order to understand the content of the film *Silmido* and the reason for such an enthusiastic response to it by Korean audiences, it is necessary to give at least a brief synopsis of the so-called "Silmido incident". In 1968, the KIM Il-sung government in North Korea was still dreaming of an armed Communist unification with the South, and as a result it arrived at the plan of having a 21-man force of armed guerillas, led by KIM Sin-jo, conduct an infiltration. Trained thoroughly as a special forces division, KIM and his cohorts broke through the underdeveloped national defense network and succeeded at bringing their attack as far the mountains behind the Blue House, the official residence of the South Korean president. Their mission was to assassinate PARK Chung-hee, then the president of South Korea, and this nefarious plot by the North Koreans, which very nearly succeeded, bound South Korean society closer once again in powerful anti-Communism. Amid this state of affairs, the Silmido force was a special division

Silmido, 2003

trained as agents to be deployed in the North, just as the KIM Il-sung government had done. Made up mostly of death-row prisoners or indefinitely imprisoned inmates, the Silmido force went through hellish training and awaited the opportunity to infiltrate the North, but with changes in the international situation surrounding the Korean Peninsula, such hard-right conservative military policy became unnecessary, and government authorities secretly established a plan to eliminate the force. Getting wind of this before the fact, the members of the Silmido forcibly seized weapons and headed instead for the Blue House, only to be stopped by military forces, whereupon they engaged in a suicide attack until cut down to a man. This was the Silmido incident.

Korean society regarded this incident as the most shameful moment of the Cold War era and for many decades refused to acknowledge what really happened. The incident only came to be announced formally as misguided government policy by the time of the KIM Dae-jung and ROH Moo-hyun administrations, which shows how open Korean society had become by that point.

It is precisely this point that KANG Woo-suk captures. Long dormant under the surface, the large-scale incident disappeared from people's memories, and the business of reevaluating it, while of course significant in its own right, was moreover well-timed commercially as well. The film *Silmido* linked with the public's increasing curiosity toward the blemished modern history of the nation at a time when the democratization process of Korean society was becoming more active, creating an explosive commercial success. This occurred because it was supported by the animalistic sense of commercial trends of KANG Woo-suk, who had honed his abilities as a director/producer.

In *Silmido*, KANG moves at a quick step. He had earned the reputation of a commercial director with socially satirical comedies like *Two Cops* and *Public Enemy*, but with this latest film, he demonstrated a new quality as a risk-taker. Rather than interpreting *Silmido* with the realist perspective of exposing hidden history, he packaged it as a Korean-style blockbuster commercial film, showing how diverse a manual of techniques for commercial success he was equipped with. The film's content deals with the Silmido incident, but at the same time it shows a different story from the incident. It deliberately breaks free from a track focusing on the incident, and instead embellishes in many parts with fiction bearing the commercial codes that audiences craved.

Rather than focusing its energies on historical context and background, *Silmido* instead directly tackles the brutal training process the prisoners assembled on the isolated island undergo to become human weapons and their treatment as subhuman individuals, reminiscent of the Nazi concentration camps at Auschwitz.

In the process, KANG groups the members of the Silmido force together as characters who are bad men, but "less bad men" who can be embraced emotionally, while designating in opposition to them the "absolute evil" of the state. Public institutions, which had been held up as the target of ridicule, criticism and accusation in *Two Cops* and *Public Enemy*, are shifted in *Silmido* to a more macro-level, substantial target at the state level. Satire and laughter had been used as a mechanism of criticism in the previous films, but in *Silmido* the laughs have been removed almost completely from the story.

Silmido is both a historical documentary in the KANG Woo-suk style and a piece of narrative "faction". KANG believes that, in order for history to become film, it can be effective if one stays within the scope of the commercial blockbuster, and thinks that this is the only way for it to get to a wider audience.

As a film, *Silmido* does not observe the rules of the orthodox historical drama, but by not doing so, it was judged to have offered an opportunity instead for audiences to approach the truth of history more naturally and with more affinity. Critics recognized it as a semi-success, but, as if to make up for their lukewarm response, Korean audiences showed their support for the film in great numbers.

Having rewritten commercial film history at a breathless with *Public Enemy* and *Silmido*, the director generated momentum and made up his mind to turn *Public Enemy* into a series. With 2004's *Another Public Enemy*, one can spy traces of his working to carry on the baton of commercial success.

As though in a conscious attempt to avoid the same story structure, the sequel comes out looking quite different from the first installment. GANG Cheol-jung, who had been the protagonist in the first film, undergoes an unusual transformation into a prosecutor rather than a policeman. His image, as well, changes from that of a loser in society to a respectable and intellectual one. By changing his outer appearance in this way, the director deliberately packages the first and second installments in the series as in fact completely different works.

With the first film, KANG had deployed skillful character comedy and enjoyed commercial success as well, but in the second film, he deliberately attempts something different. He places more weight on the story than on characters, and in the process he also pays special attention to images. Two impressive scenes in *Another Public Enemy* are a car chase scene and a gang fight among high school students, and in order to film these scenes, KANG formed a special filming unit and appointed his former second unit directors JANG Yun-hyeong and KIM Sang-jin to shoot the scenes. It is as though he intended to shoot the sequel from a completely different angle.

Nevertheless, what *Another Public Enemy* carries in from the first film and maintains the personality of is the lead character of GANG Cheol-jung. While his

Another Public Enemy, 2005

appearance is well-kept this time, GANG remains a fierce and tenacious, passionate detective who never lets go once he sinks his teeth in. But as with the first film, the events in the second film do not unfold at a rapid pace. Instead, unlike the first film, the series of crimes committed by the public enemy in the sequel have detailed aspects and are explained explicitly. As well, there is the impression that the colorful characters of the first film have been deliberately trimmed down, with the intent of focusing only on the one-on-one confrontation of the criminal and GANG Cheol-jung.

The decision to change GANG from a policeman to a prosecutor results from the criminal that he must stubbornly pursue being a slightly more intelligent and crafty character than in the first film. JO Gyu-hwan in the first film went around blindly committing murders, but HAN Sang-woo, the killer in the second film, uses his conglomerate-level school foundation to plan and carry out crimes systematically and meticulously. The director's final verdict was that the image of the loose cannon policeman from the first film was somewhat ill-suited to the pursuit of a criminal with such systematic thinking. This resulted in an abrupt change in the script and the decision to promote the protagonist into a prosecutor.

However, this decision by the director was judged by many viewers to be unfortunate. Viewers craving consistency in the series first and foremost criticized the change in the protagonist's occupation as excessively artificial.

The recasting of the *Public Enemy* series as drama rather than character comedy was another direction that viewers did not want. They still sought refreshing resolution and response to social problems through the film. The sequel saw a rare failure by the director to communicate with audiences. The subsequent reaction was that it was a mistaken response to audience wishes. Nevertheless, the film saw a certain success at the box office. This proved that expectations were high after the first film, and that the strong image of GANG Cheol-jung was still effective in the marketplace. Recognizing this, KANG Woo-suk would go back to the GANG Cheol-jung of the first film for the third installment in the series.

From *Public Enemy* and *Silmido* to *Another Public Enemy*, KANG had amassed a string of hit films that was close to the stuff of legend, but he still appeared thirsty. He was burning with the desire to make a film that would confront the audience more directly. As *Silmido* was based on a real-life incident, it was a work that depended heavily on history, and so he now wanted to make a film with a stronger sense of originality. In 2005, KANG's 15th film as a director, *Hanbando* was born from this process.

Hanbando has an interesting fictionalized situation as its premise. The film was made during the ROH Moo-hyun administration, and the president's support ratings were at their lowest. He had been showing leftist tendencies in his approach to issues related to the United States and North Korea and neo-liberalist management principles in his economic policy, and as a result faced criticism from both the right and left of Korean society. Amid this state of affairs, the one card that could put to rest criticism from both sides at the same time was the Japan issue. Japan had been creating friction with the Korean government through matters such as its insistence on territorial rights for the island of Dokdo and the issuing of history textbooks that rationalized the colonial era. President ROH adopted a hard line toward Japan, attempting to unite public sentiment.

The image of the president presented in *Hanbando* appears to have had such a figure in mind. At the beginning of the film, the South Korean president (who, unlike in reality, appears to enjoy a high level of popular support) meets with the North Korean Chairman KIM Jong-il to celebrate the opening of the Gyeongui Railroad. This railroad has a course that runs non-stop from Seoul in South Korea to Shinuiju in North Korea, but service was discontinued following the eruption of war on the peninsula in 1950. Like many things on the Korean Peninsula, the Gyeongui Railroad has become a symbol of the divided status of North and South. Thus, the reopening of this railroad means the beginning of unification between North and South. The film begins with this piece of fictional history.

However, Japan, sensing a crisis in this mood of reconciliation between the two Koreas, uses past history as an excuse to attempt to interfere. They claim that Gojong, the last king of the Chosun dynasty, gave over all property rights to the railroad to Japan. Running into an unintended political and diplomatic minefield,

Hanbando, 2006

the South Korean president enlists a single-minded historian, whom he has come to meet by chance, and attempts to show that the contract was a fraud. In order to do this, he must prove that the Great Imperial Seal with which the document was stamped was a fake, and so he issues a secret order to the historian to unearth the real seal. Meanwhile, the Prime Minister, who espouses a realist approach to diplomacy, asserts that it is preferable that war with Japan be avoided, even if it means maintaining or fixing in place the status quo of a divided peninsula. In his heart, he finds the President's doctrine of a new style of ethnic self-determination disagreeable, and he ultimately comes to oppose him on everything. When he learns that the President is secretly searching for the Great Seal, he ultimately seeks to put an end to this secret operation. Within Korea, the battle for the seal begins.

The story continues on to show South Korean and Japanese destroyers ending up in a volatile face-off in the Korea-Japan Strait. There are also scenes with fighter planes and aircraft carriers, a rare sight in Korean commercial cinema. Perhaps for this reason, the film faced the criticism that it seemed to be obsessed with Hollywood blockbusters. While this may not have necessarily been the case, at the very least there were sufficient grounds for it to be misinterpreted as a mere military action film. The fact that the director's previous work, *Silmido*, was a military film also contributed to this misunderstanding.

But when one actually looks beneath the surface, it can be seen that the film comes from a rather different place. Rather than being a war movie, it is closer to a kind of action thriller, where various internal figures in the South Korean government get swept up in a story of intrigue and betrayal surrounding the existence of the Great Seal. For this reason, the film did not meet the desires of audiences who were initially expecting another hot action film from KANG Woo-suk. But this deviation appears to have been deliberate. It seemed as though he had been told to deal with action and then suddenly come out with issues related to ideas like ethnic nationalism, but KANG had frequently shown a desire to discuss political issues directly. *Hanbando* was the film in which these typical political desires of his became apparent.

It is indeed rough, but *Hanbando* is a controversial work. There has been some difference of opinion on what ideological position the film occupies. The film is that vague ideologically. On the surface, it seems to boast excessive nationalism and right-wing racialism, ideology that is another variant of fascism.

Indeed, the narrative structure, where the entire national and ethnic destiny is wagered on a bout with Japan, does appear excessively simple at first glance. Many conservatives in Korea have regarded North Korea as the nation's chief enemy, and in *Hanbando* it looks as though that designation has simply been shifted to Japan. For this reason, there is room for criticism that the internal ideological sentiments share connections with right-wing conservatism.

But what the director focuses on more in *Hanbando* is the confrontation between the President and the Prime Minister. The message that he attempts to convey is that our enemy is not on the outside, like Japan (or North Korea), but on the inside, like the Prime Minister or the intelligence organization that does his bidding. In this film, KANG tries to communicate that the ones we should be cautious of are ourselves, what is within us.

The problem is that this is not shown precisely. It is somewhat confusing what ideological side that film is supporting. This results from the film showing entanglement in two narrative axes. It goes back and forth between one axis, the power battle between the President and the Prime Minister, and another, the conflict between the historian searching for the seal and the Korean Central Intelligence Agency agent (CHA In-pyo) who is trying to stop him. For the film to be a bit clearer, it should have united the two strands of narrative into one, or else chosen one strand to emphasize more. The right thing would have been to flesh out the story of the "conflict between the President and Prime Minister". But KANG Woo-suk neurotically attempts to balance the two stories quantitatively, resulting in a scattering of perspectives on the film. The greater discourse of looming issues in affairs of state and the smaller story showing the joys and sorrows of the historian fail to cohere, and instead clash. Indeed, a scene in which the historian meets with a member of an organization affiliated with the KCIA takes on a grotesque quality.

Ultimately, *Hanbando* was the work that showed the most ambition out of all of KANG Woo-suk's films, but it was also the one that left the most disappointment both in critical and commercial terms. Nevertheless, the film is judged to be among the films that prove that Korean cinema has evolved sufficiently in terms of genre that such a large-scale film could reasonably be produced.

KANG attempted a bold and rare experiment in Korean commercial film, but *Hanbando* is considered a failure rather than a success. After its failure, the director once again displayed his risk-taker's disposition. He decided to return to his strength, smaller films. It was at this point that planning began for *Public Enemy Returns*.

Fortunately, this film provided an opportunity for KANG to throw in all of the skills that he had developed in the course of making 15 films. Character comedy, social satire, explosive action sense—all come alive in this one film.

First and foremost, *Public Enemy Returns* succeeded once again at precisely capturing what made the series succeed. What audiences were expecting was the catharsis that comes when a protagonist with an anti-hero image, representing the lamentation of the have-nots, spews insults freely toward the haves.

The script, written by another famous Korean director, JANG Jin, places such refreshing moments throughout like land mines. The scene where GANG Cheol-jung, with his haphazard and seedy appearance, goes to take out a loan at the bank shows that KANG is once again honing the blade of his social satire. In this scene, GANG Cheol-jung lays bare his feelings about how difficult it is for a common citizen to pass through the door of a bank in capitalist society. He grumbles about how there is no reason for him to go on living as a public servant and fills his chief's desk drawer with resignation letters, but when he comes up against a grisly murder case, his passionate hero's heart starts beating again.

The major weakness of the first installment, the character of the killer, has been fleshed out in this sequel. He is developed into a slightly more sophisticated, complex character, one who in some sense appears to not be someone unforgivable, but instead to be the kind of person who can be forgiven. However, by doing this, the film comes to gain an aspect of adhering more to reality. In truth,

Public Enemy Returns, 2008

many injustices and wrongs in modern society have long since become everyday matters. The people who commit social evil go on living their lives and gaining social privileges as upstanding individuals. Through this story, the director stresses the idea that the socially powerful of this country, once you get to know them, are really villainous public enemies.

The interesting characters that appeared in the first film have also been upgraded a level, lending their support to enjoyment of the story. With *Public Enemy Returns*, KANG Woo-suk has demonstrated that his humor continues to increase. He has given his assurance that, as a commercial film director in Korea, he is a director in the present progressive, still carrying potential and practical power.

The cinematic footprints that KANG Woo-suk has left for the 20 years from 1988 to 2008 have been sufficient to leave a large mark on the history of Korean commercial film. Yet his films have been egregiously undervalued critically. For instance, *I Stand Up Every Day*, made when he had just turned 30, is a film where one can sense a sufficiently modern, present-tense quality even when viewed from the present time. That film is among the most noteworthy works of his career, but it is difficult to find any evaluation of the film in existing criticism.

KANG's films are like Molotov cocktails. They are not weapons that deal decisive blows to the enemy camp. They irritate in small increments, but they function to communicate your side's strongly held position. Molotov cocktails are sometimes considered synonymous with extremism, but in real confrontation, they will never be a match for the enemy's state-of-the-art weaponry. But they have meaning in that they are always weapons thrown by someone standing on the front line.

This is how KANG Woo-suk's films are. They stand on the front line of Korean commercial film and, like Molotov cocktails, lead the way in generating social waves. *Two Cops* was like that, as was *Public Enemy*, as were *Silmido* and *Hanbando*. But like the fate of Molotov cocktails, KANG's films have been content with the role of burning up in an instant.

There is a need to note once again how the protagonists in his films are always chaotic, non-mainstream types. The types who wield great power in Korean society politically or economically will never be the leads in KANG Woo-suk films. They will always be public enemies to him.

KANG's films therefore need reevaluation in terms of their class aspects. They may appear frantic and scattershot, but KANG has always been frank about his interest in the alienated classes: urban laborers from farming regions (*Sweet Brides*), adolescents under the yoke of the public education system (*Happiness Isn't Class Rankings, You Know*), the young unemployed (*I Stand Up Every Day*), Korean social activists such as teachers' union members (*Teenage Love Song*), rank-and-file police officers in a bureaucratic society (*Two Cops*, *Public Enemy*). As much as possible, he has aimed his efforts for the common good toward the things that films can do for the have-nots.

It is possible to view KANG's cinematic ideology as a kind of commercialization of social issues, basically a form of populism. And, indeed, this perspective has been voiced frequently. But it also seems to be the aesthetic strategy and commercial tactic that KANG himself puts forth. In fact, there are few individuals in Korean film as talented as KANG Woo-suk at inserting social material into the framework of popular film while carrying the story along so that it does not become too serious.

KANG stubbornly adheres to the idea that it is necessary to gain the sympathies of a majority of the audience rather than satisfy a minority of intellectuals. For this reason, his films have frequently gained more absolute support from the public rather than from critics. Indeed, his thirteenth film, *Silmido* set an incredible box office record in Korea, drawing more than 10 million viewers, but failed at gaining widespread support in critical circles.

Paradoxically, it is an easier course to make films that gain absolute support from a minority of critics rather than from the public. Making a popular film that the public can enjoy—the haves and the have-nots, the educated and the uneducated, all generations from adolescents to people in their 60s, all classes—could be considered a rather tricky business. The fact that social issues that could be very serious appear in KANG's films to have been deliberately established as subjects for debate to be passed over lightly may be due to the director's intention to tell his story to all people equally.

The question of how to evaluate KANG Woo-suk as a film director rather than a producer or investor is a surprisingly difficult one. Many critics in Korea would prefer to leave this question alone. This is because he is a still a director in the present tense, and it is not easy to make any predictions of where he will move on to and how he will do so. He is not satisfied with the 16 films he has made so far and continues steadily on conceiving his next work. There is a good chance that his film will run counter to expectations, that it will evolve, and that it will go on to set new box-office records and ignite discussion.

Nevertheless, critics remain stingy in their praise of KANG's films. But in spite of such low marks, the films have often generated huge box office, perplexing the critics. The people who have supported the films will feel a different kind of pleasure at this. A discussion of KANG's directorial approach, then, must be written at exactly that point and time where the perplexity of critics and the thrilled state of mind of popular audiences meet.

Thus far, KANG's films have not received attention at even the various film festivals in Korea, and they are unknown overseas because of such tendencies among critics. The somewhat unjust treatment of his films has led to an inappropriate reception for Korean commercial film. It is for this reason that a reevaluation of KANG Woo-suk and his films is urgently needed.

Interview

Interview

You are the most famous film director in Korea. You are also considered one of Korean film's most influential figures. But you are relatively little known in Europe or North America. How is that possible?

It may be a natural outcome. I took a different path from PARK Chan-wook, KIM Ki-duk, LEE Chang-dong or BONG Joon-ho. For a film director to get his name known throughout the world, he needs to get past a certain barrier. He needs to have a history of awards at places like Cannes, Berlin or Venice, or to go to places like the New York Film Festival in North America. I've never done that. I never really cared about it, and most of my films so far have been thoroughly Korean or have been aimed at Korean audiences. That may be why my films are not very well known abroad.

Are you saying that it's because your films' subject matter has been too 'Korean'?

That's not it. Well, I don't know...how should I put it? It seems to me that it may be because the marketing or publicity never expanded beyond Korea. I believed that Korean films should first succeed in the Korean market. I thought that it was important for the Korean market to grow first. In order for that to happen, I believed, commercial films had to succeed in Korea. Places like Cannes prefer more universal auteurist cinema, don't they? That's why there was a distance from what I was doing.

Is that why you're called the "godfather of Korean commercial film"?

There are a few ways to get a name for your country's films throughout the world. One way is to first produce a world-class master like Abbas Kiarostami. But the film industry in Iran is not a global one. Conversely, the power of a nation's film industry can increase, and various directors can emerge from that. I think Hollywood may be the best example of that. In our case, in the 1990s and early 2000s, our film industry assumed this vitality, and both of the ways happened at the same time. It started with IM Kwon-taek and continued on the activity of the auteurist directors I mentioned before, like LEE Chang-dong and HONG Sangsoo, and at the same time another group of commercial directors were actively leading the Korean film industry. The former group attained worldwide name recognition. The latter group played a major part in creating a boom for the domestic film industry. This includes KIM Sang-jin, as well as CHANG Yoon-hyun, KIM Yoo-jin, JANG Jin, HAN Ji-seung, and KWON Chil-in. Their names are not very well known overseas. So far, I've been at the center of that group. It's true that the leading players in Korean commercial film have led a separate existence.

Director, Producer, Investor

Is your identity as a director, a producer or an investor?

As a director, naturally. I'm nothing more or less than a director. I've always thought of it that way. But it's true that I've planned and invested in films. That may be because of the special situation that Korean film has experienced for something close to the last 20 years. In Korean film, a new current clearly formed beginning in the mid-1990s. That wave was led by people who could think of film both in terms of aesthetics and commercial aspects at the same time. Film is fundamentally an act of art, but at the same time, it's thoroughly a business. But Korean film never considered those two things as connected to each other before the 1990s. Some individuals pursued aesthetics through film, but there were also people who thought of film only in terms of business. What was the result? Neither side succeeded. But starting in the mid-1990s, and more specifically 1993, the atmosphere began to change. Expertise was demanded in both aspects. It was for that reason that I became active as a producer or investor/distributor for other directors' films at the same time as I was making my own films as a director. At that time, there were two other new producers besides myself who appeared. One of them was SHIN Cheol. He's one of the best-known producers in the Asian region because of KANG Je-kyu's *Gingko Bed* and KWAK Jae-yong's *My Sassy Girl*. Lately he's been consumed with *Robot Taekwon V*[1], though. And the other is YOO In-taek. JANG Sun-woo's *Resurrection of the Little Match Girl* and *May 18*, which was a big hit in 2007—those are both his productions. But neither of them started out as a film director. I think that at the time, I may have been the only one who started out purely as a film director and went on to do both investing and production.

1. Korean animated film about a robot, made in 1977 by director KIM Cheong-gi. It was released in a restored version in 2007. In Korea, it is currently being developed through various routes, including theatrical film, the video game industry and published cartoons.

How would you compare yourself with other foreign film directors?

I don't know. I don't think that's a question for me to answer. I hear what people say. They often compare me with the Chinese director Feng Xiaogang[2] or the Japanese director Motohiro Katsuyuki[3], don't they? Would Andrew Lau from Hong Kong or Luc Besson from France be sort of in my class? If I ever start making television dramas, will I start hearing about America's Jerry Bruckheimer? Maybe not that. (laughs) But I think that they share the same category as me in that they all have a kind of obsession, like they have to make good movies, but they also mustn't fail at the box office.

You call yourself a commercial film director through and through. What is your perspective on film?

I think we should make films that connet with many people. The name film directors of this generation, if I can put it somewhat extremely, are satisfied with just one person. Not everyone can be an 'auteur.' But depending on the time, and depending on the director, there are a lot of times where you 'play the auteur.' When I look at that, it seems like false consciousness. In most cases, we're all just 'artisans' as directors. The artisan-type director is always either ahead of or behind the public. There's just a little bit of difference in terms what he knows or doesn't know in comparison with the public. That's also the way that audiences love films. The films that many people watch are not very difficult, but that doesn't mean that they're too easy, at a childish level, either. It's exactly the level of the public itself. But it's actually not easy to know what that 'level' is. You have to get your own long history, and most of all you have to have eyes that can see the market. Many directors say about making their films, "If knowing the market situation is going to harm the film, then that's it. There's nothing to be gained from it." But that kind of

2. A major commercial film director in China. His films include *Legend of the Black Scorpion* and *Assembly*.
3. A director who is called the "man with the Midas touch" in Japanese entertainment cinema. He created the *Odoru Daisosasen*, series, which was a Japanese-style blockbuster.

talk is something for an auteurist director. A commercial film director must know a lot about how the market is functioning and operating. A commercial film director must know the importance of the market. That's the only way he can do a good job at his work as well. In any event, the type of 'artisan' director I'm talking about means someone who knows how to make films that target a majority of viewers, not just a minority of fans.

Do you have the same view as a producer and planner? For example, let's say that you have in front of you a work that is meaningful, but it's clear as day that it's going to fail at the box office, and a work that has a good chance of succeeding at the box office, but its content and level are too commercial. Which work would you choose?

I don't know. That's like asking me which one I'd pick up off the ground, a 10,000-won bill or a 5,000-won bill. In either case, just pick it up. But if the question is which one you would pick up first, depending on the situation the answer is going to be different. You would think that most people would pick up the 10,000-won bill first, but that's not necessarily the case. At times, you encounter a path to greater success when you follow the opposite course. There are a few of those films among the works that I've done investment or planning for, more so than the ones I've directed myself. A producer has to be able to really grasp that difference, and the timing.

Was it in that sense that you produced LEE Chang-dong's debut, *Green Fish*, in 1997?

I wasn't the producer. That time I was the investor. I invested the entire production cost for *Green Fish*. The producer on that film was MYEONG Gye-nam, who went on to produce *Peppermint Candy* and *Oasis* as well. MYEONG is an actor and producer, but he's a figure who is probably more famous in Europe to people involved in film than to audiences because of the films of LEE Chang-dong. We got together because of *Green Fish* in 1997: LEE Chang-dong, before he made his debut; the producer, MYEONG Gye-nam; the director and producer YEO Kyundong, the actor MOON Sung-keun, and so forth. At that time, there was this kind of atmosphere in Korean film like "All right, let's do it." Really, it was from 1997 that really noteworthy films started to come out in Korean film. Actually, viewing it from the standpoint of investing money in films, *Green Fish* was not an attractive project. And it was at a time when the name LEE Chang-dong had no meaning at all. But I thought that this film, *Green Fish*, would play a decisive role in fostering this individual, LEE Chang-dong. Actually, where it's then or today, when you do the calculations on the films by a director like LEE Chang-dong, it's almost always a minus. But is that minus a real minus? I don't think so. That's the difference between someone like me and the so-called 'corporate model' film company. The CEOs of large enterprise film companies could never make the kind of decisions someone like me makes. That's because large enterprises like that are created to pursue profit."

When you say "someone like me", what kind of person do you mean?

I'm talking about what they call a Chungmuro[4] person. Chungmuro people are people who, ever since they were young, loved films unconditionally and worked their way up from the bottom in film. The film companies that people established in that way were mostly clustered on Chungmuro, and it became such that the word "Chungmuro" became synonymous with Korean film. One characteristic of a Chungmuro person is that their interests are not always just tied up in money. Instead, it's the human network that's more important. It means that you see the possibilities for an investment more in the person than in the money. Films are definitely not made by money. They're made by people. With movies like Steven Spielberg's *Indiana Jones* films, no matter how much you throw huge amounts of money into making them, at the end of the day they were possible because of the human network of people like Spielberg, George Lucas and Harrison Ford. In that

4. Central area in downtown Seoul. Located nearby another famous area of Seoul, Myeong-dong, it was an area where film producers gathered together from the 1960s, and the word "Chungmuro" has come to refer to Korean film in general.

regard, when it comes to investing in a work, I still focus my thoughts on the person and the story. When you do that, you can sometimes invest too much, and there are sometimes occasions where the timing isn't right. In a world like the one we're living in now, someone like me is not a 100-point investor.

BAE Chang-ho's[5] 2001 film *The Last Witness* was another film you invested in.

I did. At the time, BAE Chang-ho was going through a difficult situation. When you talk about BAE Chang-ho, he was the leading figure in ushering in the Korean New Wave in the 1980s. I thought that the treatment this director received in the commercial film world as we got into the 1990s was too unkind. A director who had racked up legendary box office success at one point was now stubbornly making these independent films. Movies like *Love Story* that he had made with his own money. Other people were also saying that it was unlikely BAE Chang-ho would ever make a comeback. I didn't see it that way. When he came back into the mainstream film world with *The Last Witness*, I gladly stepped forward as an investor. That's the way that Chungmuro film people do it.

5. Noted commercial film director in Korea in the 1980s. He made 17 films, moving from realism to expressionism, and from mainstream to non-mainstream. His major works include *People of the Slum, The Last Witness* and *Road*.

So what was the result?

It wasn't successful at the box office. But even so, I think it was the right thing for BAE Chang-ho and I to make that film at that time.

How many films have you invested in or produced so far?

I've never counted them exactly. I don't know...maybe 120?

Out of those, which ones would you consider the most important?

IM Kwon-taek's *Chwihwaseon*, LEE Chang-dong's *Secret Sunshine* and LEE Jun-ik's *The King and the Clown.* Rather than saying the most important, I think it would be better to say they're the most memorable.

Why is that?

I don't know...is it because they stick in my mind as films where everyone tried to stop me from investing in them? And then, later, they were big successes, in some cases critically and in some cases commercially.

Are you a risk-taker in that respect?

If you take away the idea of gambling, the term "risk-taker" doesn't seem too far off. With gambling, you're thinking only of money and profit, but with the three films I mentioned, I had the exact opposite thought. I just believed that they would be successful.

Another IM Kwon-taek film that you invested in besides *Chwihwaseon* was *Low Life*. As I recall, that film was not very successful.

As a producer, the films that stick with you the most, and it may seem paradoxical, are the ones you work the hardest on and that fail the most at the box office. That's how *Low Life* was. That really wasn't a film that any producer could easily decide to invest in or produce domestically. Actually, it was the same with *Chwihwaseon*. Both films were cases where I invested with complete consideration of the art rather than the money. In the end, *Chwihwaseon* paid all of that back. IM Kwon-taek won the director's award at the 2002 Cannes Film Festival for that film. It was the first Korean film to win the director's award at Cannes.

Were you at Cannes then also?

I haven't been to Cannes since 2000. The Cannes festival didn't seem like something for me.

So where were you then?

I don't remember exactly. Maybe somewhere like one of my favorite street stall bars in Gongpyeong-dong, in Seoul's Jongno district?

Thinking what?

How great IM Kwon-taek is. He's made 100 films in Korea. It goes beyond the world of his films, and there are some points where you can't say anything else except that he's truly great. How can one director make 100 films? And in a place like Korea at that. It's different now, but before, Korea was not a place where films had abundant conditions in the industry aspect.

Didn't you have any other thoughts besides that?

The money that was going to come out of my company? (laughs)" (KANG Woo-suk owns Cinema Service, an investment/distribution company, and also runs the production company KnJ[6].)

In what ways do you remember *Low Life*?

Low Life, to put it simply, was a great failure. I don't like to keep using the word "great", but when I was the main investor on that film, I had the thought that it would be OK to have one film with a personal story based on the director, just like what they call a "private novel" in Japanese literature. His personal story could also be a modern history of Korean film, and in a broader sense, history itself. *Low Life* is IM Kwon-taek's "private novel" film. It was also a film with such strong virtues. But from the planning stages, I was already predicting that it would be ignored in the market. I decided to invest anyway, for IM Kwon-taek. And boy, did that film flop. (laughs) It was to the point where my whole company was reeling for a while just from that one film.

So does that mean your quality as a risk-taker was dropping?

But isn't that kind of thing really the risk-taker temperament? I think so, at least from the position of a film investor.

My Love, *Two Cops*

What is your most important film as a director?

Let me think...It's an old saying, but if you chew on all ten fingers, there isn't going to be one that doesn't hurt. But I do know which film I think was most successful

6. Production company established by KANG Woo-suk separately from Cinema Service, the investment/distribution company he runs. It produced *Welcome to Dongmakgol* and was established together with JANG Jin, director of films like *Murder, Take One*. JANG wrote the script for *Public Enemy Returns*, directed by KANG.

and which one I think was the biggest failure. That's different from saying which ones did the best and worst commercially.

Which ones are they?

Two Cops and *Hanbando*. I hear people say that *Two Cops*, which I made in 1993, was a film that became the standard dividing the "past" and "now" in Korean film. I also have a similar sense of pride in that film. *Two Cops* was a film that ushered in a new age in comedy. And compared to now, it was still a relatively repressed time socially and politically, yet it was also a film that put forth direct, explicit social satire. And it did really well at the box office. At that time, about 900,000 people went to see it nationwide, and if you judge that by today's standards, it's like 10 million viewers. It was in the theaters for something like four months, too.

Even now, *Two Cops* is funny and interesting. When the lead character, Detective JO (AHN Sung-ki[7]) goes into his house, which is listed only by an address to make it look like he's poor, his actions are hilarious. When he opens the shell of his old-fashioned telephone set and takes out a modern cordless model, and when he takes out expensive whiskey that no common person could ever afford from next to his cramped little bed.

Two Cops, 1993

That scene is funny because of the rhythm. We filmed the series of actions that he does when he goes into the room as one line of movement, and we made it have this feeling like he's tap dancing. Lightly and merrily. Of course, he's a morally lax public servant

7. Major actor in Korea. He is similar to Gérard Depardieu in France or Yakusho Kôji in Japan.

and a member of society who has a complete double personality, but we tried to show him in such a way that you wouldn't hate him. That's right. People really laughed at that part. There are still many people who laugh when they see it again.

It wouldn't be too far off to say that all of the characteristics of characters in your films are within that 'Detective JO.' Really, none of the lead characters in your successful films have been "good guys." They're just "less bad guys." People show their support for your films when those characters appear.

I've thought a lot about why that is. Is it because it's impossible from the outset for "nice people" to exist? It may instead be that the capitalist society we live in makes it so that even good people become bad. In capitalist society, living kindly means the same as living less badly. And even that almost always gives you the feeling of living your life while suffering harm because of really bad people. I mean that it gives you a feeling of relative deprivation. At that point, people resist in one of two ways. Frequently, one way in our society has been to assume a solemn expression and hold protests. Another way is to become a "slightly" bad person. So you take away the things that really bad people have, and I look at that as something like passive resistance which normal people, the petit bourgeois, all have in their hearts. That doesn't mean that these petit bourgeois types are all becoming bad people. Just to the extent that they feel a kind of catharsis through passive resistance? The older detective in *Two Cops*, Detective JO, is a guy who lives his life extorting pocket change and envelopes of money here and there on the street, but ultimately, when he's fighting with real evil, he makes his choice clear. The reason people like that character was probably because of that, the "forgivable" level of duplicity. Because nobody in capitalist society can be free from making little compromises in life.

The character of GANG Cheol-jung, the main character in your recent *Public Enemy* series, actually came from the character of Detective JO in *Two Cops*.

If you want to think of it that way, that's your prerogative. But if you only look at it that way, *Public Enemy* looks like too old a film, so I don't like that. Films are always changing, just like society changes. The *Public Enemy* series came out in an atmosphere that was totally different from the social situation of the early 1990s. To me, it's a different animal.

We've gotten ahead of ourselves here. You mentioned *Hanbando* as one of your biggest failures. I think that would also be an interesting answer.

Frankly speaking, *Hanbando* was a film where I sort of got too greedy. I don't mean in terms of the scale or the external aspects. Of course, it did have lots of helicopters, fighter planes and destroyers, which have rarely been seen in Korean film thus far. (laughs) I really did put a lot into making that film. Things like the scene about midway through where the government complex is bombed in a terrorist attack—even if the CGI wasn't the greatest, it contained things like the "flames" that I had in my mind. At the time, I thought that Japan's right wing Koizumi government was blasting our government and people in that way. But when I look back on it now, I think that I ended up getting too wound up. I put the political message too far in front. In terms of the content, even now I don't think that I made the slightest error in judgment. But, to use a common phrase, I should have "reined it in." Film is something that has communication as its basic principle, and to do that, you have to be in a position for persuasion and dialogue. You have to make people who think differently from you accept that there is a "difference." And you're not making enemies because of that "difference." As a result, *Hanbando* ended up showing too much of a nationalist inclination. And I know that's what people criticize about the film. In *Hanbando*, the political claims were strong, but it didn't provide the cinematic emotions. In that regard, it ended up as my biggest failure.

That may be the spell of the blockbuster swamp. Even when you know it's going to fail, you keep falling in. As it happens, the Japanese director Sakamoto Junji's *Aegis*, which came out around the same time, is in a similar niche.

They were probably both planned at the time when tensions between Korea and Japan were at a height. We thought that they were infringing on our territorial rights on Dokdo and printing distortions in their history textbooks, and they must have thought we were intervening in their domestic affairs. *Aegis* probably had content with right wing sentiments, like, "Let's strengthen the defense force." He must have met a fate similar to the kind of judgment I got. (laughs)

But the film had an interesting idea. In a word, it was a very cinematic concept. The mood of North and South Korean reconciliation had advanced very rapidly and the inter-Korean summit held a joint event somewhere like Dorasan Station[8]. It was an event to commemorate the opening of the Gyeongui Line, a symbol of the division between North and South Korea, but then Japan immediately intervenes. The Gyeongui Line is a railroad permanently conceded to the Japanese Empire at the time of the Chosun Emperor Gojong. Who came up with this idea?

It was an idea I developed together with the writer KIM Hui-jae, who I worked with on *Silmido*. I liked it because it was "hot" politically, but I also liked the story of the Korean history scholar who gets a secret order from the President and goes around trying to find the seal of Emperor Gojong[9].

8. Railway station midway along the Gyeongui Line connecting Seoul and Sinuiju in North Korea. It is located to the south of the Military Demarcation Line between North and South. Construction began in September 2000, following an agreement, reached at the first inter-Korean Summit between KIM Dae-jung and KIM Jong-il on June 25, 2000, to connect the discontinued line, and it was completed in April 2002. The film *Hanbando* had as its subject matter the meaning held by this railroad line in relation to the political situation on the Korean Peninsula.

9. Last king of the Chosun Dynasty, the previous incarnation of what is now the Republic of Korea. At the time of his reign, Chosun had fallen into the status of Japanese colony, and he sent a secret emissary to the Peace Conference in the Hague in 1907 to appeal to the world about the injustice of the Japanese invasion of Chosun. Despite such efforts for independence, he was ultimately dethroned. He died in 1919. His wife, the Empress Min, was killed by a group of Japanese thugs and her body burnt. This story is contained in the Korean musical *Myeongseong Hwanghu*, and it is also recreated as a flashback in KANG Woo-suk's *Hanbando*. There are also theories that Gojong's death was the result of Japanese poisoning, but these have not been proven.

But around the time of the film's completion, it turned into a story that people were always hearing through real television and newspaper reports. That's why *Hanbando* was unlucky.

Maybe the reason why the work on the film was so interesting can be found in that. The film couldn't be too far removed from reality, but it couldn't be too close either. The situation changed so much for *Hanbando* between the time we started the story and the time we finished filming. It ended up looking like *Hanbando* had just copied the political news. But strictly speaking, truly coincidentally, reality followed the film.

The story structure of the film, where they go "all in" with the fate of the nation and the people in a fight with Japan, at first glance really does look too simple. It might have been better if you had instead focused on the "internal fight" between the President (AHN Sung-ki) and the Prime Minister (MOON Sung-keun[10]) over the issue.

That's right. It was there that it lost its balance. I should have emphasized the story rather than the spectacle. Midway through, I got a bit excited. But it isn't the case that *Hanbando* had right-wing commercialist intentions like people in some quarters say. Instead, the political purity of my attempt to break the commercialist mold made the film's direction unclear.

Why were you unable to hold yourself back?

I'm a bit of a fiery person. It's my weakness that, once I start running forward, I don't do a very good job of looking behind me or next to me.

10. Major actor in the Korean film world along with AHN Sung-ki. He has appeared in many films of a strongly political nature, including PARK Kwang-su's *A Single Spark*, which portrayed labor problems in Korea under the PARK Chung-hee government during the 1970s, and JANG Sun-woo's *A Petal*, which depicts the political aftereffects of Korea's popular unrising in Gwangju. During the time of the ROH Moo-hyun government, he served as vice-chairman of the Korean Film Council, a national film policy organization. He formed a relationship with KANG Woo-suk through films such as *I Only Want to Live to 20*, *Green Fish* and *Hanbando*.

At times like that, someone should be next to you giving you words of wisdom. Is it possible that the fact that you're an influential producer and investor makes it so that you can't hear the sound of your real feelings?

I often hear that kind of criticism. But frankly speaking, that may be a concern that you feel the same way whether you're in Hollywood, in Europe or, like me, someone who does both directing and business at the same time here in Korea. If you open your ears too much, you can't do your film. Ultimately, you end up caught in the system. If you close your ears too much, the business of film doesn't work. The system collapses. So everything is a question of balance, and there isn't anyone yet who realizes that perfectly. I'm not like Clint Eastwood. I'm still a long way from gaining that kind of discernment and insight. I'm still just someone in the process. At times I succeed, and other times I fail. At times, I'm a good producer, but there are also occasionally times when I'm not.

Public Enemy, My Destiny

Let's talk about your most recent endeavor, the *Public Enemy* series. The Korean title of the third work is not "Part 3", but *GANG Cheol-jung: Public Enemy 1-1*. What is the meaning of that?

At the time of the first sequel, I changed the main character of GANG Cheol-jung a bit. Actually, I didn't change the character; I just changed the bit about his job. In the first film, he was a detective, and in the second he appears as a prosecutor. He's imprudent, a troublemaker with a loose cannon personality, but he has a burning sense of justice, and in that sense, he didn't change too much. But there were ultimately some artificial aspects in changing him from a detective to a prosecutor. Maybe because of that the reality of the story in the second film lost something. So in the third installment, I returned the main character to his original form. So in terms of the meaning, it's not so much a story going from Part 1 to Part 2 to Part 3;

instead, there's a strong sense of it being a sequel to the first film. So I used the expression "1-1."

It seems to mean that the second film was a failure.

I wouldn't say it means it failed. It means that the first and third films are at different places. Nothing more or less than that.

If you look at the series as an extension of *Two Cops*, you see the poster for *Public Enemy Returns* and they use the expression "the fierce guy vs. the bad guy." There's no "good guy" in this film either.

In some ways, I tried to emphasize that this film's story doesn't follow a dualistic structure of good vs. evil too much. The story where good and evil fight and the

Public Enemy Returns, 2008

good guys end up winning is too simple, isn't it? And too didactic. The protagonist in my film doesn't have a superhero image. Instead, it's closer to the image of an antihero you seen in an American underground comic. They're not stylish, and they have these complexes inside. They're people who are more used to the darkness of the world than the light. They fight bad guys, but if you look closely into the process of their fight, they're really not that different from the bad guys.

GANG Cheol-jung, the main character in *Public Enemy*, is closer to a gangster than a detective.

But detectives are really like that. They seem more like gangsters than detectives. They seem like gangsters who defeat gangsters. Of course, the character of GANG Cheol-jung is presented with more of the dramatic elements of a human, but it seems like that contributes all the more to Korean audiences feeling a paradoxical sense of reality. I might say they feel something like vicarious satisfaction, catharsis, through GANG Cheol-jung, because he just speaks for all the feelings they have inside.

How did you come to start this series?

In a sense, I might say that it expresses a kind of social rage that I had pent up inside of me. When you live in this world, you come to experience a lot of truly absurd things. But in many cases those things use the framework of legality, and in many case they are dressed up as myths of social success. However, in most cases, they have that kind of social wealth and power, but actually also have a lot of problems morally. That's the problem within Korean society. It's a society where the idea of noblesse oblige doesn't really operate that much. A society where you should dedicate yourself and serve the common good, but in reality many people are public enemies. All societies have cases of that, but it's been an especially big problem in Korean society to date. With this *Public Enemy* series, I was aiming it at those kinds of people.

One of the strengths of your successful films, like *Two Cops* or the *Public Enemy* series, is the abundance of supporting characters on the periphery. In *Public Enemy*, characters like the third-rate thug San-su (LEE Mun-sik) and Yong-man (YU Hae-jin) do a good job of adding flavor.

You could call it a characteristic element of character comedy. Funny episodes are created out of the image of various characters caught in ironic situations and floundering. For example, that's how it is in the scene n the first *Public Enemy* film where the neighborhood lowlife San-su gets hauled in by GANG Cheol-jung and interrogated. The chief detective (KANG Shin-il) blatantly fabricates evidence that he says was used in a robbery, and from San-su's perspective, he can't do anything about it. Actually, San-su didn't steal anything, but if he just goes on denying it, he'll end up involved in a bigger crime of assault or murder. So he bites the bullet and owns up to the crime that the detectives have 'created', because from his perspective that's the best thing to do. How awful must that be? It's something that detectives shouldn't do, but audiences probably take the side of the detective or the chief when they see that scene. We get an odd kind of laughter from a reality where you something have to use expedients to do the right thing. It's because in one sense it's refreshing.

Those figures also play important roles in *Public Enemy Returns*.

What's funny is how those characters end up forming these kinds of bonds with the main characters, and it's because, once you really see things, with the exception of the really bad guys, we're all more or less the same in the way we live our lives. You can sense something like the way normal people lives their lives in that. That's why people like that kind of unseemly character.

The *Public Enemy* films are also among your megahits. What meaning do they have to you?

As a commercial film director, if I made a film that was loved by many people, I don't think there's any greater meaning than that. And at the same time, I also think that I did a good job in my own way of fusing social messages into the framework of commercial film. I feel a sense of pride in that they brought together the popular and the social, that they were fun and at the same time meaningful.

Entering the Film World with *Mrs. Emma 2*

There are some peculiar films among your filmography, namely *Who Saw the Dragon's Claws?* and *Bedroom and Courtroom*. Let's talk a bit about these films. They come from a different place from *Two Cops* and *Public Enemy* and from *Silmido* and *Hanbando*.

As a director who makes commercial films, I have thought that we always have a weakness for certain genres of films. One of those is the serious political film. Actually, in our case, we had no choice, because until the late 1990s Korea was not a country where freedom of expression was perfectly guaranteed. Politically, we suffered under the military dictatorship for a long time and endured acts of censorship, not only external censorship but also censorship within us, in terms of political expression. Under those conditions, no proper political film could be made. If there were films made before that, it wouldn't be too far off to say that they were mostly anti-Communist films or films with content that accommodated the system that had anti-Communism as a national policy. For that reason, my feelings when making *Who Saw the Dragon's Claws?* in 1991 were, "Let's do something a little bit shocking. Let's break this complex we have about not being able to make political films." It was a film where I tried to faithfully realize the political film thriller they talk about so often, with the big opposition party politician's sex scandal, conspiracy and betrayal between ruling party Assemblymen, and the resulting murder.

The script was by the director KANG Je-kyu[11].

Yes. At that time, KANG Je-kyu was working more on writing scripts than on direction. In a way, you could call this film something of a dry run for *Shiri*, his big hit film as a director.

If you look at the film, it really resembles the political situation in the early 1990s in many ways.

Not necessarily. There's no need to view the film in terms of the political situation in Korea in one particular era. A movie can't work just being particular to a certain era. It needs to contain a universality generated in our human society. *Who Saw the Dragon's Claws?* is a film that can be viewed in that context. I wanted to say something about the fossilized ethical consciousness in the political world. I wanted to say directly that our politics is really corrupt. They present this grand, righteous mission of doing things for all the people, and I wanted to say that the true nature of their political acts was that they actually came from personal desires and the resulting intrigue and betrayal. For that reason, *Who Saw the Dragon's Claws?* may look different on the outside, but it shares a lot of commonalities with the threads of *Two Cops* or *Public Enemy*. It's like that in that it aims at our society's taboo consciousness. If there's a difference, it's that I revealed the humor completely [in the later films].

It didn't succeed very well with the public.

It's the same case now, but in Korea, political thrillers never succeed at the box office. That's probably because our political reality has more dramatic aspects than films do. In the early 1990s, that kind of atmosphere was stronger than now. It

11. Considered one of the leading commercial film directors in Korea along with KANG Woo-suk. His films, including *Gingko Bed*, *Shiri* and *Tae-guk-gi*, have functioned as a kind of milestone in the history of Korean popular film. *Tae-guk-gi*, like KANG Woo-suk's *Silmido*, drew approximately 12 million viewers in Korea.

Who Saw the Dragon's Claws?, 1991

was a time that stood as an extension of the 1980s, and people probably didn't want to experience uncomfortable political realities in film too. But for a commercial film director, that aspect is always a dilemma in terms of choosing political material. That's because I think that stories that deal with political intrigue can give the greatest pleasure as material for commercial films. But turning that into a story that goes beyond the real political situation is another thing altogether. I think that the failure of *Who Saw the Dragon's Claws?* can be found in that aspect.

How was it in the early stages? At that time, were you oriented more toward black comedy like *Two Cops* or toward legitimate political dramas like *Who Saw the Dragon's Claws?*

I don't think it was any intention of mine to make comedies. Because the time when I came to decide that I had to make films was when I saw LEE Chang-ho[12]'s *A Windy but Pleasant Day*, and I thought, "Wow, they have movies like that in Korea. I've got to make films like that." But I didn't have any intention of making my films with a heavy and rigid feeling like orthodox political dramas. The films that I enjoyed watching and was influenced by in middle and high school were things like HA Kil-jong's *March of Fools* and *Byeongtae and Yeongja*. So I think that from that point, I thought I should make films that were fun.

12. Leading figure in the Korean New Wave movement in the early 1980s. His debut was a melodrama, *The Stars' Heavenly Home*, made in 1974, but afterwards he made noteworthy films about social issues. His major works include *A Windy but Pleasant Day*, *Declaration of Fools* and *People of Dark Streets*.

I heard that you dropped out of college to make films.

I went to college for exactly one year. I did 16 months of life in the army, came back and went back to school before dropping out after six months. And I went straight to Chungmuro.

Did you quit school because you weren't a film major?

My major was English literature. I didn't quit school because of my major. Almost none of the Korean directors of my generation were film majors. Nearly all were non-majors. Anyway, I didn't think it was the time for university studies. I thought I needed to get to Chungmuro and study directing as fast as possible.

Did you have any kind of family history to make you have such a 'yearning' for film?

I became aware of film early enough that it wouldn't be too much of a stretch to say that I was stuck on it from my childhood. My mother was a big influence in my becoming that way. At that time, it was a somewhat conservative age. My mother would often go to the theater, and when she went she would take me as a "hostage." I think that my mother dragged me to see almost all of the Cinemascope films that played in Korea. *Ben-Hur*, *Lawrence of Arabia*, things like that. Nowadays they've either almost completely disappeared or they've lost their influence, but when I was young, I was a regular at theaters like the Danseongsa, Piccadilly, Myeongbo and Segi[13], which at the time were the major theaters in central Seoul. Then the Bruce Lee craze, which was like a rite of passage if you were a film fan in Korea, came and went for me too, and when this young kid who thought only of film went to university, there was no way any other studies were getting in. Most of the time I was in the library, but I wasn't studying for my major. I was usually writing scripts.

13. The largest theaters in Korea until the 1990s. They were on streets close by each other in downtown Seoul, creating a large audience draw. All were single-screen theaters.

No matter how much of a film fan you may have been, it couldn't have been easy to enter the film world. How did you realize that dream?

The surrounding relationships formed naturally for that, for me to follow the path of a director. My older brother being an actor in action films was a big help. Because of him, I came to meet certain people, and one of them was the director JEONG Ji-yeong, who is still working today. At that time, JEONG Ji-yeong[14] had just started making a name for himself with *The Mist Whispers like a Woman*. If LEE Chang-ho was the one who made me a film director, JEONG Ji-yeong was the one who really got me into the film world. JEONG Ji-yeong's help may have been the biggest. Big enough that I consulted him about dropping out of school. He's not doing very much now, but the film critic PARK Pyeong-sik[15] provided decisive help in my starting out in film. With so much help from different people, I was able to get onto the production team at Chungmuro relatively easily. My first work was doing preparation for *Mrs. Emma 2*[16] under the director KIM Haeng-su. That was around 1984.

So it was with *Mrs. Emma 2* that you began making films in earnest?

But the planning for that film was canceled midway through. I heard that the director JEONG In-yeob later remade it. Actually, the first film that I really got involved with was a publicity film for the Defense Ministry. It was a half-documentary, half-theatrical film made by the director LEE Yeong-sil in 1983. At that time, there had just been the incident where First Lieutenant LEE Woong-pyung[17] came over from North Korea into the South in a MiG. It used that incident

14. Director who made his debut in 1982 with *The Mist Whispers like a Woman* and went on to receive praise for works such as *Nambugun (The Southern Army)* and *White Badge* that depicted the Korean War and Vietnam War from a progressive standpoint. Another of his major works was *The Life and Death of the Hollywood Kid*.
15. Korean film reviewer active in the 1980s and 1990s
16. A leading series of Korean soft-core adult films made in the 1980s. 13 films were made all together. It was an odd series made in the situation of the 1980s, where freedom of expression with regard to social and political themes was suppressed under the military dictatorship.
17. High-ranking North Korean Air Force officer who in 1983 flew into South Korea on a MiG. In South Korea, he advanced to the rank of colonel in the Air Force before becoming a professor at the Air University. He died in 2004.

for the story, and the actress in it was YANG Mi-kyeong, who would become very popular for the TV drama *A Jewel in the Palace* [18].

So how was life as a production staff member?

People are a bit skeptical about this, but in comparison with other Korean film directors, I didn't spend too much time as a production staff member. In a way, I did just one, and that was *Mrs. Emma* again. This was Part 3. Someone I met at that time was the director JEONG Jin-woo [19]. I'm still close with this veteran director because of our connection at that time. After that, I worked on the production staff for one more film, though I think it would be more correct to say that I was a second unit director rather than a staff member. It was a film called *Seong Isuildyeon*, directed by LEE Seok-gi, and it was maybe 1987 when I did it. And I made my debut as a director in 1988, a full four years after I came to Chungmuro. Putting it in terms of working for a company, it would be considered a very fast promotion.

Before your debut, you were greatly influenced by LEE Chang-ho. It doesn't appear that you ever did actually work under him.

Of course, I did go visit LEE Chang-ho. I got a lot of help in many ways by doing that. But I never had the opportunity to work under him. Rather, he saw my first film and actively suggested that we work together. At the time, he had his own film company, called Pan, and after I made my debut I worked there for a while. Then, when I finally came to work together with him on something, it was the time of

18. TV drama about Jang-geum, a woman who rose to the rank of palace cook, the highest position for a woman in the Chosun Dynasty. It was very popular in Asia and Eastern Europe, and was something of a leading work in the so-called 'Korean Wave.' The actress who played the lead, LEE Young-ae, would appear in films by director PARK Chan-wook, including *Joint Security Area: JSA* and *Sympathy for Lady Vengeance*.
19. Director who dominated Korean film until the 1980s, enough so that just the films he directed amount to some 50 films. He commanded substantial influence in the Korean film world at the time, working as a director, producer and theater owner. In 1988, he showed *Fatal Attraction*, a UIP direct distribution product, for the first time in a theater he directly operated, assisting in the advancement of Hollywood into the Korean market.

Who Saw the Dragon's Claws?, which we talked about before. The person he brought to see me was none other than KANG Je-kyu, who was a screenwriter at the time. LEE showed me the script and said, "You're the only one who can make this film, Woo-suk." In a sense, *Who Saw the Dragon's Claws?* was a film planned by LEE Chang-ho.

Why do you think he said you had to make the film?

It must have been because of my first film, *Sweet Brides*. People misunderstand it because it's such an old film, but *Sweet Brides* was not a romantic comedy. In a sense, it was a pure social drama. I came to make that film because one morning, I opened up my eyes and saw a newspaper, and the headline said "Rural Bachelor Fails at Marriage with City Woman, Kills Self." I slapped my knee and said, "Now that's a movie." So I made the movie. It dealt with the story of city and village, rich and poor, which our society was going through at the time in the 1980s. It must have been because it was that kind of film that LEE Chang-ho brought me *Who Saw the Dragon's Claws?*.

Sweet Brides, 1988

So in a sense, you really did start by making films that dealt with social issues.

I often employ humor and comedy as a way of dealing with social issues in film. But when it's the reverse, when the comedy carries the story along, it needs to have social issues underlying it for the true flavor to emerge.

Most of your early films are like that: *Sweet Brides, Happiness Isn't Class Rankings, You Know, I Stand Up Every Day, I Only Want to Live to 20...*

I Stand Up Every Day may appear a bit different from the rest. Originally it was called *Baegilmong (Daydream)*, but the title was too uncommercial, so I changed it. It's a film that people consider a failure, but it isn't really. It's a black comedy about a social issue of the time, the problem of the unemployed, slackers. With my early films, there are the films themselves, but they're also important because of the people who got together to make them. It was then that I met the people who are like "my family" and whom I continue to work with today. The film planner LEE Chun-yeon[20] and the actor MOON Sung-keun are both people I met at that time, and with whom I continue to make films even now.

Becoming #1 in Korean Film's Power Rankings

You are celebrating exactly 20 years of life in film this year in 2008. How would you separate your career in film by time period?

I've never divided it up that way, but maybe it would be something like this: From my debut in 1988 with *Sweet Brides* to *Two Cops* in 1993. That time was like a youthful apprenticeship period. My dreams and passion were at their biggest then. And then,

20. One of Korea's leading producers. He produced *Saminjo (Trio)*, an early film by PARK Chan-wook. His major works include the *Whispering Corridors* series of horror films and director CHANG Yoon-hyun's *Hwang Jin Yi*.

following the success of *Two Cops* I set up my production company, KANG Woo-suk Productions[21], so from then until 2000. During that time, I did a lot of production work for other directors' films rather than doing my own. That was a time when a new atmosphere was being created in Korean film, and when Korean film was preparing for major changes as an industry, and I think I was at the center of that. In 1997, I expanded KANG Woo-suk Productions and set up the investment and distribution company Cinema Service. And then from 2000 to 2004. At that time, I was able to link up with foreign capital and large sources of capital. I joined forces with the American capital Warburg Pincus[22], and later I hooked up with another source of financial capital and ended up making the large company Plenus Entertainment.[23] Cinema Service became an affiliate of that group. It was a time when I was really becoming a "big wig", but frankly speaking, it was the most painful period for me. Korean cinema was being shaken by money games then, and in the process I too got hurt a lot and had a very rough time. It was then that I got a new sense of how films are not money but a business done by people. And finally from 2004 to the present. I parted ways with the big capital and went back to my company, Cinema Service. In general, I think it can be divided up into those four periods.

In a broad view of things, the 20 years from when you started work as a director in 1988 to now in 2008 have been a period of great changes for the Korean film industry. You are a living witness to those changes.

That's right. For the past 20 years, I have been right at the middle of the major changes experienced by Korean film. There were good times and bad times. Since

21. KANG Woo-suk made a huge splash in Korean film with the making of *Two Cops* under this film production company, which the director established in 1993. This company is considered, along with Shin Cine and KiHweck ShiDae, to have ushered in the age of the producer in Korean film.

22. American private equity fund company.

23. Large entertainment group formed in 2002. It consists of Cinema Service, the production/investment/distribution company led by KANG Woo-suk, along with the film production company Sidus, the recording and management company Sidus HQ, the record production and wholesaler/retailer Yejeon Media, the film investment and distribution companies Chungeoram and IM Pictures, the film set and equipment lending company Art Service, the multiplex theater chain Primus Cinema, the broadcasting production company KIM Dong-hak Productions, and the management company Max and Company. In 2004, it was absorbed into the Korea's major distribution company, CJ Entertainment.

2007, a sense of crisis has been surging within Korean film, but the reason I don't feel that way is because I have witnessed several situations. Korean film doesn't collapse easily. Its frame is relatively well woven together, its infrastructure is solid, and most of all it has an abundant pool of human resources. The last part is particularly important, because in the end film is made by people. Among my younger friends, there are lots of passionate film buffs, and most of all the students who are coming out of university film departments all over the country. Just in the Busan region, where they hold the Busan International Film Festival, there are more than 10 universities with film departments. I think that as long as we have these young human people to work in the field, the future of Korean film is not at all dim.

Speaking with you about the history of Korean film over the last 20 years has been another interesting endeavor.

Really? I'm not sure how my own history overlaps with modern Korean film history. It just seems like I went through a lot of major events.

Looking back, what kind of cycles do you think there have been in the film world?

I agree with what you've been talking about, the theory of 10-year cycles in Korean film. In a broad view, it seems like film changes around an axis of ten years. Of course, that's not an objective approach. But to people like me, who have worked in the film business with a considerable amount of "sense" and instinct, it feels like there are areas where the changes of 1997 and 2007 connect with the changes of 1987. In 1987, around the time when I released my first feature film, *Sweet Brides*, the Korean film world was suffering because of the "UIP direct distribution controversy"[24]. It was at the time when Hollywood major distributors were

24. This refers to the protests and demonstrations that Hollywood major studios encountered in 1988 in the process of directly distributing films in Korea. The previously discussed director JEONG Ji-yeong was among those leading anti-Hollywood protests, and there were other incidents, including the release of a snake in a theater run by director JEONG Jin-woo and the detention of individuals in the film world.

entering the Korean market directly, and UIP was at the forefront of that. I think the first film was *Fatal Attraction*, with Michael Douglas. At the time, the Korean film world, in a word, went crazy. There were all kinds of protests everywhere. The director JEONG Ji-yeong, whom I've always come to think of as a big brother in film, was even detained because of that. It's something that's tough to imagine now. That's how intense it was. Everyone predicted that the Korean market was going to collapse. Really, the Korean market went through rapid structural changes with a starting point around 1987 to 1988.

The Korean film industry did go through severe changes, but it didn't collapse. Why was that?

It was because they had the screen quota system[25]. UIP started it, and then Hollywood majors like 20th Century Fox, Warners, Sony and Buena Vista came in one after the other, and [the screen quota system] was a certain defense system to protect Korean film, which was relatively weaker. It was a system that had an "obligatory number of Korean film screenings", saying that they had to show Korean films for 146 days out of the year.

Was it ultimately the Hollywood majors that led to the modernization of the Korean film industry?

When I think about it now, it seems like it was a delicate choice. Frankly speaking, before the majors came in, our distribution and circulation systems were somewhat pre-modern. I think that the advancement of Hollywood into our market may have been one factor in the advancement and specialization of the Korean film industry. But usually in such cases the domestic market gets completely eroded by Hollywood. One example of that is South America. You can see that just looking

25. System of obligatory numbers set for the screening of Korean films. Until 2007 in Korea, theaters were required to show Korean films for 146 days per year per screen. The system was intended to fight market erosion by Hollywood films and protect domestic films, but in 2007, under intense American pressure, the number of days for obligatory screenings was reduced to 76, effectively abolishing the system.

at how Hollywood controls close to 80% of the world market. But in our case, we've been making use of a kind of protective trade strategy, the screen quota, at the same time for the last 20 years. I think that it was really most effective, because the result was that, at the same time as we were bringing in things from the advanced nations, we were nurturing capital for domestic film that would be able to stand on its own. Direct distribution by Hollywood major studios was a double-edged sword for us. We basically guided them to use the good side of the sword.

However, the screen quota system has now actually been discontinued. So do you think that there is a deep connection between the abolition of the screen quota system and the slump in the Korean film industry?

You can look at it that way or not. It's true that, thanks to the screen quota system over the past 20 years, the native Korean film capital that is Chungmuro has grown enough to stand side-by-side with Hollywood, at least domestically. In particular, the entry of large enterprises into the film industry has performed that role. For that reason, it's true that the screen quota system as well demanded changes from the past. But the problem is that film is by nature a business with a lot of ups and downs, and when the situation in the film market is taking a turn for the worse, there really is no strategy for protecting the market once the quota system has been discontinued, as is the case now. So another way might be to apply the obligatory number of Korean film screenings at a flexible rate, adjusted to the market situation, rather than applying it uniformly. For example, raising or lowering the quota percentage according to the market share of Korean films. In that sense, Korea's screen quota system should be reexamined, with an eye toward continuing it rather than discontinuing it.

Before, you said that you agreed about the 10-year theory for the Korean film industry. In 1997, the IMF economic crisis hit Korea hard. At the time, film companies were going bankrupt left and right. How did you fare?

To put it simply, at that time, there was a hollowing phenomenon with investment capital. Both domestic capital that had just entered the film industry and large companies like Hyundai and Samsung immediately pulled out of the industry. Everyone suffered in the process. But, when I look back on it, it really was also a substantial learning experience. At the time, bad capital, speculative capital, had entered the film world, if only for a short time. With that experience, we all came to share the knowledge that you should not associate yourself with capital that is trying to turn film into speculation, no matter how much you feel like you have to make films. So-called finance capital, bad financial capital where money is gathered in obscure ways—that kind of money muddied up the waters in the film world. It took about 2 years for that kind of capital to get out completely and for the film world to return to normal. And since then, however difficult the conditions may have been, mega-hits started to appear. Things like KANG Je-kyu's *Shiri* and PARK Chan-wook's *Joint Security Area*. It was then that Korean film started to come back to life.

How was your situation?

I went ahead aggressively. It was then that I expanded my existing production company, KANG Woo-suk Productions, and created the investment and distribution company Cinema Service. The situation wasn't good on the outside, but I thought that at times like that, it was all the more reason to keep good quality commercial films coming. So rather than directing myself, I focused my energy more on production, investment and distribution. I went in on a lot of films, as the main investor or partial investor, you name it. I regarded myself as a kind of pipeline, channeling in capital from different sources. That was the time when director LEE Myung-se's film *Nowhere to Hide* was made, letting people the world over know about PARK Joong-hoon[26]. That was a film I distributed. After that, I made films like CHANG Yoon-hyun's[27] *Tell Me Something*, LEE Jung-gook's *The Letter* and *Jagwimo (Ghost in Love)* which could be called one of the first Korean films to use special effects, the first form of fantasy film—all during that time. I also made romantic comedies like *Love Bakery*. Two other films that came out at that time were HAN Ji-seung's *A Day* and *A Masterpiece in My Life*, another film starring PARK Joong-hoon. Some of them I distributed directly, some of them I invested in, and others I did simple distribution for. Some were successful and some were bombs. I think that I was living like a crazy man at that time. Like an independence activist. It's a strange thing to say, but that's really how I felt at the time.

In the process, you came to hear yourself referred to as "the most powerful man in Korean film."

I think that was when I really started to hear how I was more of a producer,

26. Another leading Korean actor along with AHN Sung-ki. He played the lead in KANG Woo-suk's *Two Cops*. After his performance in LEE Myung-se's *Nowhere to Hide*, he appeared in Hollywood director Jonathan Demme's *The Truth about Charlie*.
27. Director of *The Contact*, an early film by Cannes Best Actress award winner JEON Do-youn. He has directed many films, including *Tell Me Something*, *SOME* and *Hwang Jin Yi*.

investor and distributor than a director. Ultimately, that moniker came to become a major burden to me as a director. I think that at the time I was more passionate about non-directing work than directing work. And my distribution company, Cinema Service, was also entering a new phase. What I learned then was that in film distribution, you have to manage a large number of films with a plan, even it means having a mixture of successes and failures. I thought you needed to have a lineup of about 12 to 16 films a year to maintain a distribution company with domestic capital that can match up with Hollywood majors in word and in deed. At that time, I had really aggressive ideas and was overflowing with confidence. I had distributed 20 films just in 2000. With those kinds of numbers, I had exceeded the distribution numbers for Hollywood major studios in Korea. So the stuff about "the most powerful man" got louder and louder. That's what I thought at the time. I thought that we needed to have our own distribution network to put out Korean films even if the screen quota system disappeared, and I thought that I was going to make that network.

It was at that time that you received an investment of 20 million dollars from the British venture capital firm Warburg Pincus.

I needed money. Like I said before, in order to have an investment and distribution company with a certain degree of scale, I needed a lot of money, because in order to maintain a number of films to distribute, I needed to grab these films beforehand through early investment, whether as a main investor or partial investor. It was difficult procuring that kind of money domestically. Even if it were possible, a lot of it was bad finance capital. While I was worrying about this and that, it was Warburg's Hong Kong office that contacted me first. And the terms of the contract were pretty favorable to me.

In order to get that way, you must have had a number of opportunities.

It's heartbreaking what happened to the film, but I started to have that idea strongly when I was deciding the investment and distribution for PARK Kwang-su's[28] *The Uprising*[29]. That's a story from 1998. Around that time, we were just starting to emerge from the IMF shock, and the finance capital in Korean film was still making its voice heard here and there. With the film *The Uprising*, these finance capitalists all withdrew their investment. I heard that they were telling the director, PARK Kwang-su, and the then-producer, YOO In-taek, to do this and that about the content and direction of the film. Looking at that, I thought, "This isn't good. If they can do that, the film is going to get twisted to suit the taste of finance capitalists who are only interested in getting paid, who are bent on speculative profits and don't care about film." That was why I took the investment from Warburg.

At the time, your "power in film" continued expanding. You are also in charge of many in-house productions.

I wouldn't necessarily say "in charge." I'd say that there came to be more production companies forming loose forms of affiliate relationships. As it happened, my investment and distribution company, Cinema Service, needed a large number of films, and from the standpoint of the production companies making movies, they needed a stable source of funding. In a sense, it was a kind of natural partnership created between people who wanted to go on making Korean films in Korea, and not people who wanted to import foreign films. The production companies I worked with at the time included Cine 2000, Koo @ Film, C&Film, Joheun Yeonghwa, Director's Home, Dada Pictures, Cineworld and Taewon Entertainment. Some of them are still active, and some have gone out of business. When I look back on it, that was our high point. Not just for Cinema Service, but for all of Korean film. This kind of "let's go" atmosphere that was just

28. Figure who, along with JANG Sun-woo, spearheaded the Korean New Wave in the 1990s. Major works include *Chilsu and Mansu, A Single Spark* and *Geu Seom-e Gago Sipda (I Want to Go to That Island).*
29. LEE Jae-su led a popular uprising on Jeju Island in 1901. Born a commoner, he resisted corrupt bureaucrats and the Catholics who did their bidding. The film *The Uprising* portrays this story.

overflowing. It was a time when we had a kind of faith that Korean film was not going to be dominated by Hollywood in the world film scene, that there was going to be a situation where we could make the voice of our own film culture heard, and that we were going to make it that way.

Around that time, Korean film was going through a renaissance period.

Yes. Around 2001, 2002, 2003, there was a lot of talk about how Korean film was going through a renaissance. In particular, there were a lot of people overseas seeing it that way. It was probably because of a lot of notable auteurist films had come up from directors like HONG Sangsoo, LEE Chang-dong and KIM Ki-duk, but in the background, it was because there had been a solid growth of the commercial film arena. As an industry, Korean film grew in leaps and bounds during that time. For example, at the time I was making *Two Cops*, the total annual audience numbers for Korea were around 20 million viewers. But after going through this period, it's grown to 170 million viewers now in 2008. In terms of production costs per film as well, the old average cost for commercial films, one billion won, kept growing, and now it's reached 5 billion won. A little over 10 years ago, nobody could have imagined making a film that cost 10 or 20 billion won. But I heard that KIM Jee-woon's *The Good, the Bad and the Weird*[30], which was made a little while ago and got good reviews at Cannes, had a total budget of more than 20 billion won. Viewed from Hollywood standards, 20 billion won may correspond to a lower-budget film, but viewed in terms of the Korean market it's a huge blockbuster. Korean film has reached that level thanks to the foundation formed in the "good times" of the early 2000s.

The development of the Korean film industry in leaps and bounds, and the rapid growth of audience numbers in particular, may have been greatly influenced by multiplexes, but

30. The latest work by KIM Jee-woon, director of *A Tale of Two Sisters* and *A Bittersweet Life*, it opened at a gala screening at the 2008 Cannes Film Festival to good reviews. The title of this film quotes Sergio Leone's 1966 western *The Good, the Bad and the Ugly*, starring Clint Eastwood.

I'll leave that for later. One thing I'm curious about is whether *The Uprising*, which you invested huge amounts of money into in 1998, was a success or not.

It was a huge failure, so much so that the company was reeling from it. It's really ironic. When I have affection for a film and put effort into it, it seems like it's sometimes that much more of a disaster. There are a few of those films in my career. *The Uprising* was like that, and IM Kwon-taek's 2004 film *Low Life*, which we talked about before. Right after *Silmido*, which has a huge hit drawing more than 10 million viewers in 2003, I invested in a martial arts fantasy film called *The Legend of the Evil Lake*, and it too went that way.

Which means that, as a film investor, your batting eye for projects is not 100 percent.

You're right, but you could also be wrong. Both *The Uprising* and *Low Life* were films that I predicted would fail and invested in anyway. I just didn't know that they would lose that much. The important thing is that I thought that sometimes those kinds of films need to be made, regardless of whether they lose money. I think that way because I don't think of film as just a business, and because I began as a director. Of course, after bombing so hard, you inevitably become more cautious about several things. But even now I don't regret investing in those films.

But even after a failure big enough to rock the company like that, you have always appeared to get up again.

It's really amazing. So I think that in the film business, you have to follow your luck to a certain extent. The failure of *The Uprising* was offset by director KIM Sang-jin's *Attack the Gas Station!*[31], which I invested in at almost the same time. The failures of *Low Life* and *The Legend of the Evil Lake* were made up for by

31. 1999 film by KIM Sang-jin, a former assistant director to KANG Woo-suk who has become another noted commercial film director in Korea. It's a raucous comedy about four losers who seize a gas station.

Silmido and the first *Public Enemy* movie, which I made myself directly before and after. With the film business, you're also putting your goods out there. The fact that I have no regrets even when I have a failure may be because I know the cycle. I learned not to go from joy to sorrow every time I repeat failure and success because I've experienced those things repeatedly.

What is money to you?

It's kind of like a mirage. Viewed from the Korean perspective, I'm a film entrepreneur who's earned a whole lot of money. Sometimes I've made tens of billions of won just on one film. But I've never actually touched that money with my own hands. Most of the time, it goes away the second it gets deposited in the bank because of some film that's in the red. So paradoxically, I have no concept of money. The money I earn from film ends up going into film. For that reason, I have to restore the money I earn from film with film. The most important thing, whether you're a film director, a producer or an investor, is whether you can make the next film. Because that's the only way you can sustain your life in film. If someone who makes films doesn't use the money he earns for films, but spends it on his normal life, he's ultimately giving up on living through film. As a director, as a producer, there's nothing so unfortunate as that.

Around 2000, you were something of a "godfather" to producers at film companies that had formed a partnership with you and to directors. Do you have the temperament of a boss?

This is my philosophy of film investment. Don't invest looking at individual films, invest looking at the person and at the production company. Isn't that right? The film business is totally a business of connections. Isn't Hollywood the same way? The Weinstein brothers most likely don't decide their investments looking at individual films, they do it based on works by directors whom they've had a long time to judge. So people sometimes do a good job and sometimes they don't. When they don't, you have to encourage them, and when they do, you have to push them on so that they can do even better. I may have adopted the business practice of considering human relationships important because I was a director myself. It was a natural partnership that emerged from the relationships with younger and older friends who were all in the same boat with me at Chungmuro. It could also be interpreted as a somewhat peculiarly Korean situation. Of course, I'm not going to deny that I have the temperament of a boss.

But in the process, you've also been criticized as a '"monopolist."

That may not be something that occurred because of the relationships formed between my investment and distribution company and other production companies. It was closer to a horizontal relationship than a vertical one, because we were giving and receiving help based on each other's needs. I started to get criticized as a monopolist when I got involved in things like the theater business and film set businesses, because what looked like a vertical organizational structure had started to appear.

A Season of Ambition

Starting with Warburg Pincus in 2000, your film capital has gone through constant ebbs and flows.

I kept needing large sums of money. In the process, I ended up making frequent M&As with capital sources. I don't feel the need to discuss every last detail. When I think about it now, it was a kind of money game. I tried hard not to get mixed up in that, and I think that I kept what I needed to, but there were also a lot of side effects from the battle of large amounts of money going back and forth. Things started to snowball in 2002, when Locus Holdings took over Cinema Service through a stock swap with Warburg Pincus. In the process, Cinema Service became part of the Plenus Entertainment Group. It had become an affiliate. And as I was forming the Plenus Group in that way, I really entered the multiplex business. It was then that I started making the Primus theater chain.

Beginning with your work in the set industry, you also got involved in the post-production business, including advertising and marketing.

It was also at that time that I made a company called Art Service. With the creation of the large umbrella of Plenus, a vertical organization of film business occurred naturally. The idea was that we would unify the entire process from making the film to marketing it and putting it out on the market with a kind of one-stop service concept, centering on Cinema Service, which invested, distributed or directly produced films, and extending to Art Service, which covered the later stages, and to the theater chain Primus. I didn't have any other reason for being interested in the theater business. It was because it had become an environment where, if you didn't have a theater, you ultimately couldn't go forward freely with film distribution because of the multiplexes operated by large corporations. I thought that I absolutely needed theaters where my movies, the movies we invested in, could be circulated safely. But after I did that, I started to get criticized in the Korean film world as having monopolized the industry too much. It's a reasonable criticism, but I thought that it was a way of standing up to Hollywood, and of standing up to the market ruling structure of the large corporate film companies that had recently grown domestically.

The Cinema Service Group, connecting Cinema Service, Art Service and Primus, didn't last very long.

It was dissolved in 2004 when Plenus Entertainment was taken over CJ Entertainment. And just before then, I had succeeded in separating Cinema Service from Plenus. In a way I only narrowly managed to get Cinema Service back. After that, there were a few slowly progressing conflicts. Primus was ultimately sold off by CJ. Art Service remained as a company operated together with CJ. I got hurt a lot and I learned a lot when I was going through the Plenus business. Looking back on it, I left myself wide open for it. The important thing is that the film business should never enter into a money game structure. The moment film companies go into the stock market, they get influenced by the daily fluctuating stock prices. Every time you make a film, you end up worrying what influence its success or failure will have on stock prices, and thus whether you should do it or not. Like we've been talking about, the film business must be free from that kind of cyclical structure. The moment you invest in a film or come to make a film while looking at the money, that film—even as a commercial film—loses its vitality. Of course, you also have to have that structure. For example, thoroughly planned films like Hollywood blockbusters are going to be like that. They're films that are made aiming at a particular season and particular audiences, with custom-made stories so they can predict profitability. That kind of market also has to exist. But I thought that wasn't something for me. To me, that kind of film is like hatching a fish. The commercial films I made are like fish that I pull directly from the sea. Sometimes the sea is calm, but sometimes there's a typhoon. Fishermen like me may have a hard time predicting things, but we have to be the people facing the sea and pulling out fresh fish. In the process of Warburg turning into Plenus Entertainment, and Plenus deciding to sell off to leave a greater profit, I too felt like I was becoming a slave to the big payday. So I took it upon myself to make an exit from that structure. There were a lot of twists and turns, but when I think about it now, I think it was a natural outcome. I'm a person who enjoys making movies, not someone who is happy just getting rich off them.

Why do you think you got lost in that kind of illusion?

When you work in the Korean film industry, you end up in a situation where you can't help getting involved in the theater business. It may be because of personal ambition or a constant desire for capital, but in one sense it's because of structural peculiarities of the Korean film industry. In this country, the majority of a film's sales structure is made in the theaters. It's a severely distorted structure. 85% of a film's sales come in the theaters, and at best 15% in additional copyrights. If you compare it with the US, you can see how serious it is. As far as I know, in the US, when you make a film, about 40% of sales are made at the theater, and the remaining 60% are made in other areas besides the theater, that is, in the additional copyright market. But in Korea, the DVD market has not succeeded in growing. The video market is totally dead. Even in the TV market you can't make much of a profit. Basically, the theater ends up being the only way of surviving. In that situation, the more you earn at the theaters, the safer you feel. A fast road to making a lot in the theaters is showing the film in as many theaters as possible at the same time when it opens. If you do it that way, you can prepare a break-even point in the theaters. Of course, doing it that way, you can also have some huge bombs. But you end up with the idea that it's the best way under this distorted sales structure. That's why they prefer the wide-release distribution method[32] in Korea. But what do you have to do to ensure that many screens? Having my own theater would do it. So all the big film companies own multiplexes.

So you have controversies over screen monopolies and oligopolies.

I often get caught up in that controversy, because my films premiere on some 400 to 500 screens. (The total number of screens in Korea is about 1,700—Ed.) So I know all about how some of the film scholars are raising criticisms about how we need to forcibly limit the number of screens. This problem must be resolved. But before limiting the number of screens, we need to clean up this film sales structure that is concentrated only on theaters. If the percentage of sales earned at theaters drops from 85% to 90%, where it is now, to around 50% to 60%, the phenomenon of screen monopolies will naturally decrease. It's extremely difficult, but we need complex and difficult efforts to reorganize the system. It's not an easy story. There are so many troublesome issues with the Korean film industry because we have to solve several problems at the same time to solve this one problem.

What is the situation now for the film work you've been doing besides direction?

I'm focusing once again purely on making films and distributing them. My investment and distribution company, Cinema Service, still has a lot of influence, and it's maintained a strategic partnership with the major investment and distribution company CJ Entertainment. But I am debating now about whether to focus on distributing like I did in the past. The situation has changed a lot. I'm operating a separate production company besides Cinema Service, a company called KnJ. With that company, I'm joint director with the young director JANG Jin. He was the one who wrote the script for my latest film, *Public Enemy Returns*.

32. Method of getting as many screens at possible early in the release of a film to draw audiences. Because of this method, a major method of major distributors, there are frequently controversies over monopolistic and oligopolistic methods.

He's made hit films like *Guns and Talks* and *Murder, Take One*. So far I've been playing the role of investor in JANG Jin's films.

How do you view the future of Korean film?

Korean film has gone through a lot of ups and downs in the last 10 years. It seems like yesterday when the domestic market share reached 60%, which was really a period of continuous victories. At the same time, it's also fallen to less than 10%, like it has recently. What does this mean? It shows the film industry always goes back and forth between heaven and hell. Directors really don't need to be so sensitive about changes in the industry, because it's enough for them to just work hard making good films. But I'm a producer, and a planner, so I can't help worrying about changes in the industry. Film is a culture and an industry. I see both sides at the same time. Viewing things in that respect, I still think that Korean film has hope, because there are lots of outstanding filmmakers. But I also think that now is time when Korean commercial films have to get a lot of notice. So far, it's been mainly the auteurist films that have gotten the notice, but that's one part of Korean film. There are more films with a stronger popular quality.

What have you been working on following *Public Enemy Returns*?

I decided on one film for investment. It's by a talented young director, LEE Hae-jun, who made his debut with a film called *Like a Virgin*. The title of it is *Gim Ssi Pyoryugi (Mr. Kim's Drift Diary)*. For the past year or two, I had halted my investment in films. JUNG Jae-young, who stars in my film *Public Enemy Returns*, introduced [the film] to me, telling me one day that there was this enjoyable script. As soon as I read it, I decided to invest all of the production costs. In the Han River in Seoul, there's a placed called Bam Island. It's a very small island in the middle of the river, and this woman lives there in seclusion. The story happens when a man attempts suicide by jumping in the river and ends up drifting to this island and meeting the woman. It was the first time in a long time that I really enjoyed reading something. It felt like an original comedy. I also saw possibilities for success. Anyway, I plan on starting with this film and getting a bit more into investing in and planning films, and into producing films.

Any personal works?

I haven't decided on anything yet. The one thing that is clear is that I'm not going to do a big budget film like *Silmido* or *Hanbando*. I talked about this at the beginning, but with those two films, I was unable to infuse them very well with humor, which they say is my strong point. I acknowledge that. I look at them now and wonder whether I didn't have any room for that. I was too wrapped up just in the filming. When a film gets to a certain scale, you feel so tired just from the preparations. So you end up just shooting it according to the script or according to the storyboarding, frankly speaking. There are parts where it doesn't look like I had any real ideas, and there are parts I just gave up and moved on because I was tired. It's unfortunate and I regret it. But if I make another big film, will I repeat the same mistakes? Maybe I can't. I think that big films are like clothes that don't fit me. What I really do well is talk about a big universe through a small universe. That's easy, and it's fun. But *Silmido* and *Hanbando* were films that talked directly about the big universe. I don't want to take on that burden again. I'd like to make a light political satire set in my hometown, Gyeongju. I haven't decided on the title. And...my children are going to school in Vancouver, in Canada. And my wife has gone with them. I often go back and forth between here and Vancouver, and I sometimes think that it wouldn't be a bad idea to make a film about a father who lives apart from his family like me.

How do you see yourself in 20 years?

There are lots of old veteran directors in Japan. I heard that Oshima Nagisa made a movie like *Taboo* when he was 67, in something like 1999. Imamura Shohei was making movies up until a few years before he died, when he was 80. He was so old and decrepit that it was hard for him even to shout "action", so maybe his assistant directors did it? In 20 years, I won't be past 70 yet. I wonder whether I won't still be spending time on the film set with the staff members then as well. I hardly know how to do anything except make films.

Are you happy as a film director?

There may not be another director in Korea as happy as me. I have made a name for myself, and I'm proud of playing a role in really developing the film industry in various ways, whatever ups and downs there may have been. But as a director, I always get the feeling that I'm about 2% short. That's how a director is. He always feels like he's not good enough, like he's hungry and thirsty. He always has something like a feeling of crisis, like this film might be his last. I'm the same way. If this film, *Public Enemy Returns*, doesn't succeed, I may be done as a director. In any case, with this film, I got the opportunity to continue being a director. I'm grateful just for that. So I'm happy.

Biography

Biography

He speaks like a fast-talking Seoulite, but surprisingly enough, KANG Woo-suk was born in Gyeongju, in North Gyeongsang Province. The old capital of Korea, this city was the seat of government for the ancient nation state that existed from around 500 to 700 A.D. and for the Silla kingdom. Even today, artifacts and ruins are being unearthed throughout the city. It is also a region where people use a heavy dialect of Korean that is different for even other Koreans to understand.

The fact that KANG Woo-suk's home was this center of splendid classical culture also shows how conservative the environment was in which he grew up. Indeed, KANG's personality as an individual has a somewhat conservative quality that contrasts with the political and social issues he presents in his films. It can be surmised that these circumstances of his birth created a temperament that finds sex issues between men and women embarrassing. It is exceedingly rare to find any sex scenes or love scenes in his films, and this tendency has frequently formed the basis for criticism from Korean feminists that he is a macho male fundamentalist.

But KANG Woo-suk's background of origin assumes a somewhat complex aspect. His parents were born in Hwanghae Province, located in the north central region of the Korean Peninsula (in what is now North Korea), and migrated southward as North Korea adopted communism. His father made a great deal of money operating a match and chemical factory in Gyeongju, enough that the cartoonist LEE Hyeon-se[1] would remember KANG Woo-suk as "the son of the richest man in Gyeongju."

Based on the family's solid financial status, KANG and his siblings (two brothers and two sisters) began studying in Seoul at an early age, and KANG Woo-suk, the youngest son, transferred to Segeom Elementary School when he was in the fifth grade. He later attended Cheongun Middle School and Myeongji High School. These schools are all located with Seoul's four main gates, and show that KANG's early years were spent in a relatively well-off environment.

As an elementary school student in Gyeongju, KANG made a name for himself with his ability to do calculations in his head. At the time he was in elementary school in the 1960s and early 1970s, mental arithmetic competitions were popular in Korea, and he is remembered to have represented his school. In his childhood home, there are still plenty of the certificates, medals and plaques he won in his childhood at such competitions. He was that quick with calculation from an early age, and people say that he was a clever child.

His career as a calculation king, paradoxically, has thus far functioned as a reason for him not to get particularly close with advanced digital machinery like electronic calculators, computers or the Internet. He is known as an 'analog' individual, something unique in today's Korean society, and he is famous for not using the Internet, which seemingly ever other Korean uses.

His math abilities have also created frequent episodes in Korean film. They would often have light-hearted contests, where numbers in the 100 million to billion range would be lined up on a full sheet of A4 paper based on addition, multiplication, subtraction and division, and KANG would compete with someone

1. A major Korean cartoonist. His work *Gongpo-ui Oeingudan* was adapted into a film called *LEE Chang-ho's Baseball Team* in 1986 by director LEE Chang-ho.

using an electronic calculator to see who could calculate faster and more accurately. Every time, KANG would finish immediately and wait for his opponent to finish. His opponent would marvel at KANG's ability, faster than the time it took to press the buttons on the calculator and more accurate.

His speed with figures is another element explaining KANG's personality. It suggests how the director, who has done work such as investment and the theater business in addition to film direction, is that fast at making decisions and pushing projects forward. Of course, as a result he also endures failures and difficulties, but it also shows how KANG's film work possesses a dynamism greater than that of others in the business.

In some aspects, this special skill of being able to calculate and put in order the workings of the world more quickly than others also drove KANG to become someone with a somewhat "hasty temperament." A youth where he enjoyed wealth greater than middle-class homes, pride in having greater intellectual ability than others, and his rash personality—all of these forced KANG to make choices uncommon in Korean society. They led him to drop out of college: he spent just one full year in the English department at Sungkyunkwan University before quitting in his second year. He had made the judgment that, instead of studying a fixed academic curriculum at the university, it would be better to go right to the scene as soon as possible and learn film. In Korean society, whether or not one has graduated from college is still a very important element in deciding one's social status. For KANG to drop out of school meant that he was that confident in his future life in film, and at the same time showed that he had the disposition of a risk-taker, which had already long since become a kind of nickname for him.

The figures encouraging him to follow the path of film appear to have been his own family members, especially his mother. A former nurse, she is known to have had an open personality, unlike KANG's conservative father. She hoped that her children would develop their own special talents rather than follow the path of graduating from an appropriate university, going to work at a big company and living as a salaryman.

It appears obvious that KANG was able to accumulate cinematic knowledge as a

child thanks to his mother. She was a film buff, and took her son to see Cinemascope films like *Lawrence of Arabia*, *Ben-Hur*, *The Sound of Music* and *Gone with the Wind*, allowing KANG to nurture his own dreams of film naturally. Once he entered university and he came to blow off school and head more in the direction of film, his mother didn't try to hold him back, but instead encouraged him.

It may be gathered that this quality of KANG's mother also had an effect on his second brother, Yong-seok, deciding to become an actor in action films. Long before Woo-suk debuted as a director, Yong-seok was working from 1980 as a leading actor in Korean kung fu films like *Aegwon (Love Fists)*, *Women's Fists* and *So Aegwon (Little Love Fists)*, which were already on their way out. Later, KANG Yong-seok would become a major partner in his brother's work in the film business, and at one point he also managed large multiplexes in the Daegu and Gumi areas.

The fact that his brother was an action film star in some ways actually does explain how the opportunity was provided for KANG Woo-suk to easily become close with people in the film world. Before he made his debut, KANG Woo-suk was already forming friendships with established figures in film, and it was at this period of entering the film world that he met people like the film director JEONG Ji-yeong and the critic PARK Pyeong-sik, which whom he maintains friendships to this day.

It is true that such personal relationships functioned to some extent in KANG's ability to go through a relatively short training period, rare in the Korean film world, and make his debut in 1988 with *Sweet Brides*.

KANG's first practice work was made during his period of military service. Doing his army life for 16 months at the rear line in the Ministry of National Defense, he participated on the production staff for a military promotional film made by director LEE Yeong-sil. After leaving the military and dropping out of school, he came to work as an assistant director on a series of soft-core adult films. They included *Mrs. Emma 2* and *Mrs. Emma 3* [2], and afterwards KANG's status

2. In the 1980s, Korean film was subjected to severe censorship by the CHUN Doo-hwan military dictatorship, and freedom of creative expression was fiercely suppressed. The films that the government allowed at the time were Japanese A/V sex films and soft-core adult films. The *Mrs. Emma* series of films made during this time was produced as part of an industry strategy to protect itself.

would rise somewhat, allowing him to work as assistant director on films like *Seong Isuildyeon*, by director LEE Seok-gi, and *School Days*, by LEE Mi-rye, a rare female director in Korean film.

He started out in film doing somewhat 'peculiar' projects like the *Mrs. Emma* films, but his dreams were somewhere else. The foreign films that he is known to have assisted in translating when he was working as an assistant director showed that he was dreaming of making films in a different place in the Korean film world as it passed through the 1980s.

From 1984 to 1988, he found work translating foreign films to get through the poorly-paid life of an assistant director. He is known to have worked on the translations of films like Milos Forman's *Amadeus*, John McTiernan's *Predator* and Tsui Hark's *The Swordsman.*

KANG's ability to debut as a director in a relatively short time, without having to go through great difficulties, owes itself to the human relationships he quickly formed, but it also can be attributed to a creative sensibility that read new currents in the Korean film world of the time.

For his first film, *Sweet Brides*, the support of KIM Il-woo, an actor of solid standing who raved about the script, played an important role. The film company Sewon Films, which no longer exists, invested an amount corresponding to 200 million won in today's terms. The script for *Sweet Brides* was written by KIM Sung-hong, who was working as a teacher at Seoul's Gyewon Girls' High School. To make the film, KANG convinced KIM to quit as a teacher. Quitting the school for a director making his debut, with an uncertain future, KIM went on to do work with KANG for a rather long period of time. He also directed *Well, Let's Look at the Sky Sometimes*, a sort of sequel to KANG's early hit film *Happiness Isn't Class Ranking, You Know*, and also wrote the script for KANG's major work *Two Cops*.

Sweet Brides was not a big success at the box office, but it gave KANG a soft landing in the film world. Most importantly, it proved the impetus for the director LEE Chang-ho, whom KANG regarded as a spiritual mentor, to go and seek out the young director. LEE would also participate as an essential figure in the planning of KANG's fifth film as a director, the political thriller *Who Saw the Dragon's Claws?*. The script for that film was by KANG Je-kyu, the director who would solidify his position as a commercial film director in Korea with *Shiri* and *Tae-guk-gi*.

Following the period of his debut, KANG Woo-suk began to enjoy a string of popular successes. His second film, *Happiness Isn't Class Rankings, You Know*, allowed him to solidify his position as a commercial film director early on. This film depicts problems related to the university entrance system, a specifically Korean situation, and the story of children having the golden age of their youth arrested by these issues. Comic, yet with a tragic ending, the film ignited an explosive reaction among young viewers at the time.

The film's producer, LEE Chun-yeon, has remained a longtime friend and mentor to KANG Woo-suk and shared a cinematic friendship with him. He cannot forget the powerful emotions of the film's premiere. It opened in 1989 at a theater on Toegye-ro, a street near Chungmuro, where films companies are clustered together. In front of the box office, there was an endless line of teenaged viewers who had come to see the film. LEE recalled the experience, saying, "I sensed that a hungry period for both of us had ended. Most of all, I sensed that we could now make the movies we wanted." His prediction was on target. The words "Happiness isn't class rankings, you know" went beyond a movie title and became something like a rallying cry for people pursuing real happiness. Many still speak the title of KANG's old film when they pursue the value of a higher happiness than material wealth.

Having established his ability as a popular commercial film director with the making of *Happiness Isn't Class Rankings, You Know*, KANG came to gain the explosive support of a broader age group of viewers beginning

Happiness Isn't Class Ranking, You Know, 1989

with *Two Cops*, which is considered to be his major work. The film uses a comic touch to portray a corrupt and incompetent, but human, policeman. It was with this film, made in 1993, that the words "greatest commercial film director" came to be attached to KANG Woo-suk's name. Two more films would be made in the *Two Cops* series, and direction for the third was done by KIM Sang-jin, who had started out as an assistant director for KANG.

With the success of *Two Cops*, KANG launched his own production company, called 'KANG Woo-suk Productions.' This company would later play the role of a kind of birthing room for new Korean commercial films and the major talents attached to those films. The aforementioned screenwriter-turned-director KIM Sung-hong, KIM Ui-seok, director of *Man with a Gun*, and countless producers all started out at KANG Woo-suk Productions.

With the establishment of this company, KANG dived actively into work as a film producer and investor. He would go on to dissolve KANG Woo-suk Productions in 1997 and establish the investment and distribution company Cinema Service, starting on the course of a true film entrepreneur. The films he invested in, produced and distributed during this time include LEE Chang-dong's *Green Fish*, KIM Sang-jin's *Attack the Gas Station!* and CHANG Yoon-hyun's *Tell Me Something*. KANG himself was not so successful at making notable films of his own. His works at this time included *Bedroom and Courtroom*.

From 2000, his film career came to resemble the period just before a storm. Entering the arena of investment and distribution with Cinema Service, KANG started drawing in huge amounts of financial capital through his film company, ultimately functioning to bring about outward growth for the whole of the Korean film industry. From 2000 to 2004, the finance capital he came to work with would include the American company Warburg Pincus and the Korean companies Locus Holdings and Plenus Entertainment. Through this process, he brought in large amounts of money and greatly increased the number of films he invested in and distributed, coming in a single leap to hear himself referred to as the most powerful man in Korean film. But KANG himself remembers this period as the most difficult and painful time for him as a film director, as he ended up getting caught in what he calls a "money game."

In the midst of this process of developing the shape of his business, KANG the director stunned the film world with a series of hit films. The first *Public Enemy* film was made in 2001 and enjoyed huge popularity. He would go on to make *Silmido*, based on the taboo topic of the North Korean infiltration agents[3], boasting of passing 10 million viewers for the first time in Korean film history.

Silmido made KANG Woo-suk indisputably the most influential man in Korean film. In the period around the making of this film, films that he had invested in and distributed, including IM Kwon-taek's *Chwihwaseon* and LEE Chang-dong's *Oasis*, began achieving noteworthy results representing Korean film at international film festivals.

Following *Silmido*, KANG would take on the challenge of another large-scale Korean blockbuster, making the massive "faction" spectacle *Hanbando* in 2006, but its results were unsatisfactory in terms of both criticism and box office. He scaled his course down to "small films" once again by following *Hanbando* with his latest work, 2008's *Public Enemy Returns*, which was met with a warm welcome by Korean audiences. Once again drawing a total number of audience members in excess of 4 million people, the film came to assume a place on KANG's list of successes.

KANG is currently conceiving his next film while going back and forth between Korea and Vancouver, where his wife and three children live. For the next ten years, he plans to focus his energies on making his own films. In order to do this, he has cut down the scale of Cinema Service, his investment and distribution company, and expanded the scale of operations for his production company, KnJ.

3. During the long period of the military dictatorship, the South Korean government did not acknowledge the truth about South Korean agents being sent north, unlike the spies being sent south from North Korea. Silmido is the name of a small island off the coast of Incheon where South Korean agents received training in actual fighting conditions. The film *Silmido* tells the tragic story of the special force, which led a military rebellion when faced with elimination by the South Korean government. The South Korean government would first acknowledge the truth of the infiltration agents in 1998 under the KIM Dae-jung government.

Synopsis

Synopsis

Sweet Brides (1988)

Small town friends Jae-su and Go-saeng want to marry women from the city, even going as far as to participate in a matchmaking event sponsored by a social group in Seoul, but they meet with repeated failure. The two of them decide to look for brides while living in Seoul. Go-saeng gets a job as a deliveryman for a supermarket, while Jae-su works as a janitor at a women's health club. Jae-su ultimately falls in love with Chu-ja, who works as a masseuse at his health club, but he is rejected even by her for being a small-town bachelor. Meanwhile, Go-saeng likes Yeong-ju, who works in a tea room, but he fails at winning her love because of Dae-cheol, the delinquent who lusts after her. Dejected, Jae-su and Go-seong decide to return home, but Go-saeng summons up the courage to rescue Yeong-ju from Dae-cheol and flees with her on a motorcycle. Just then, Chu-ja comes running, saying that she wants to go away with Jae-su.

Happiness Isn't Class Rankings, You Know (1989)

Bong-gu and Hyeon-jae, eleventh graders in high school, have the lowest grades in class and are troublemakers to boot. Bong-gu secretly has a crush on a classmate, Eun-ju, but she, unlike him, is a top student who is always ranked first in the class. What is getting in the way of Bong-gu's love is grades. Hyeon-jae dreams of becoming a film director. He has a crush on the school nurse and satisfies his impossible love for her by making amateur films. One of their classmates, Chang-su, helps his mother and studies hard in spite of his family's difficult financial situation, but Mun-do, who comes from a rich family, always mocks him. Meanwhile, Eun-ju, even as she continues to be first in the class, feels suffocated by her parents, who are always emphasizing only her studies. Instead, she sneaks out of the city with Bong-gu and enjoys puppy love instead of studying in the classroom. But the result is that she falls from first in class to 17th, and, despairing at this, Eun-ju ultimately throws herself to her death from the roof of her apartment.

I Stand Up Every Day (1990)

JANG Baek-su has succeeded at graduating, barely, from a second-rate Seoul university that he attended thanks to his parents, who sold their country rice paddy to put him through school. But there is no work for him to do in society. Not one place will hire him, and as though trying to flee from this cold treatment by society, he joins the army and spends some time there, but even after he gets out nothing changes for him. He even gets defrauded when he thinks that he's getting a job. Failing repeatedly at getting a job, he ends up with the label of a two-time failure. Baek-su would like to finally get a job, become a dutiful son to his elderly parents and get married with Eun-sil, who lives alone next door to him, but reality does not go the way he wants. Another figure of torment for him is Mr. YUK, the boss who tries to seduce Eun-sil with money. Mr. YUK even goes as far as to use violence to force Baek-su to drop Eun-sil, but Baek-su refuses to back down and tries to protect her.

Teenage Love Song (1991)

Jun-seok has been branded as a bad student. One day, he stands up to his teacher Je-cheol, but ends up with an invitation to his teacher's home instead, and he starts to open his heart a little. Jun-seok is gradually more and more attracted to Chae-ok, another student with a vivacious personality and pretty face, and Hyeong-su, the bookish boy who knows about Jun-seok's feelings, helps him get close to her. Meanwhile, Je-cheol suffers through days of torment when a colleague of his is fired because for joining the teacher's union. But one day, he too ends up fired because of a subjective answer question submitted by the students on a test. The students, including Jun-seok, Chae-ok and Hyeong-su, begin to feel anger about the school's actions against the teacher and start a commotion.

Who Saw the Dragon's Claws? (1991)

With the presidential election two months ahead, KIM Ji-won, a famous anchorwoman for the KBC broadcasting station, leaves a secret rendezvous with PARK In-gyu, her married lover, who is a candidate for the opposition party. As she leaves, she witnesses a murder. The next day, it is revealed that the victim was Assemblyman JEONG Yong-uk, a powerful ruling party candidate and former martial law administrator, and everything turns upside down. But the public prosecutor concludes that the Assemblyman committed suicide over because of his family situation and ends the investigation. Meanwhile, two reporters, CHOE

Jong-su from KBC and KIM Hyeon-su from the Hanbit Ilbo, discover that the Assemblyman's death is connected with the presidential election and with a kind of conspiracy. KIM Ji-won struggles with her conscience as a reporter, which dictates that she disclose what she saw, and the blow that this will deal to her lover PARK In-gyu in his candidacy. Ultimately, she reveals the truth anonymously through her colleague CHOE Jong-su by tipping off KIM Hyeon-su about what she saw. The political and popular situation goes into deep turmoil, and in the process KIM Ji-won goes missing. To save her, CHOE Jong-su compromises with the group behind the plot and prepares a revised broadcast saying that JEONG was not murdered, but committed suicide as was originally announced by the prosecutors.

I Only Want to Live to 20 (1992)

Late night radio DJ Hyeon-jun first hears the name MIN Cho-hui from Cheol-su, who has come to visit him on his way home from work. Cho-hui is an 18-year-old girl with bone marrow cancer, and she is eagerly awaiting the broadcast of a letter telling her story on Hyeon-jun's program. The letter contains pure and beautiful sentiments and moves Hyeon-jun, who reads it every night on his program. Listeners hearing the show send warm feelings of comfort for Cho-hui's sadness, and she comes to feel more attached to life. But her pain gets worse, and despite her earnest wish just to make it to the age of 20, her foreshortened life keeps moving toward its end. Watching this with sadness, Hyeon-ju prepares a charity concert called 'For MIN Cho-hui.'

Mister Mama (1992)

Childish father Hyeong-jun is half-conscious from the drinks of the night before. He gets up in the morning and discovers that his wife has left home and that their newborn child is bawling. The wife fancies herself a progressive modern woman, and when Hyeong-jun discovers that she has left him and the baby, he doesn't know what to do. He makes a fuss changing diapers and feeding the baby for the first time, and he even ends up going to work with the baby. Meanwhile, Hyeong-jun's wife, having resolutely abandoned the man and child who were only tying her down, declares that she is going to live a new life, and when she meets a seemingly perfect man she gloats that her decision was right. But as the new man gradually begins to show his true colors, she realizes that she isn't where she's supposed to be.

Two Cops (1993)

Veteran detective JO is not a bad guy, but he is the stereotypical corrupt cop making a living shaking people down in his jurisdiction. He has a philosophy of life stating, "What's good is good," and he dodges major incidents, but one day he finds himself partnered with new recruit Detective GANG, who stubbornly adheres to the rules. With divergent personalities and views on life, the two detectives clash on everything in their partnership, but the veteran is consistently frustrated by his young partner's stubbornness. One day, a beautiful woman named Su-won comes and asks Detective GANG for help, saying that an unidentified man is threatening her. He ends up visiting her apartment, and as comes to like her more and more, he begins to abandon his parochial personality. But this is all part of Detective JO's strategy to change him by using the wiles of beautiful woman. Amid all of this, the two detectives get their hands on a crate of drugs and get into another fight over how to deal with it. GANG brushes off JO's attempts to stop him and goes alone into the hideout of the drug organization. He thinks that Detective JO has high-tailed it, but just as his life appears to be in danger, the older detective shows up and the two of them take the organization down.

Killing My Wife (1994)

Bong-su and So-yeong run a film company together, with him as the boss and her as a planner. They love each other madly and get married, but their married life turns out to be far different from what they dreamed of. Unlike Bong-su, who absent-mindedly passes over everything, So-yeong is meticulous and stubborn and always tramples over his opinions. Sick of his wife, who is like a policewoman at home and work trying to get control over everything, Bong-su ultimately attempts to restore his masculine confidence by having an affair with Hye-ri, the star of the film he is producing. But he knows exactly what will happen when So-yeong learns of this, and he wants to get married again with Hye-ri, so he ultimately arrives at the conclusion that he must kill his wife. He uses various means to try to do her in, but every time he fails, and in the end he enlists the services of a professional killer.

Two Cops 2 (1996)

Detective GANG was a passionate detective when he first joined the force, but he has suddenly found himself living like the older partner he always hated, Detective JO. A new detective joins the force: Detective LEE is full of ambition and passionate about justice, just like GANG used to be. LEE is disgusted by GANG's disgraceful actions on everything and tries to compel GANG to resign. Having lost his comfortable lifestyle and the ability to do as he pleases because of Detective LEE's actions, GANG tries to put him in a difficult position by giving him unsolved cases of violent crime. But contrary to GANG's expectations, LEE wraps up many

of the cases in short order. As a last resort, GANG tries the beautiful woman trick that Detective JO had used on him in the past, but even that doesn't work with LEE. Amid all of this, a thief gets caught robbing the house of a high-ranking official, and in the process of the investigation GANG snatches a diamond, but he ends up discovered by LEE. GANG has a dilemma. As a condition for staying quiet about GANG's criminal action, LEE forces him to solve a bunch of violent crime cases.

Bedroom and Courtroom (1998)

CHU Hyeong-do works so hard with his many duties that he can never make it home on time, but he ends up getting suspended. His wife, full-time homemaker LEE Gyeong-ja learns of this and decides to file a lawsuit. Her suit demands compensation for herself as a neglected wife from the company her husband worked for, Ilsan, claiming that her husband neglected his duties in the bedroom because of his excessive workload at the company. Gyeong-ja entrusts her case to the lawyer MYEONG Seong-gi, who has become a star as a professional divorce counselor on TV, but when she gets to know him, not only dose she learn that he is an immoral attorney who only knows about money, it is revealed that he is also the corporate lawyer for the Ilsan company. The person who comes to the rescue in this difficult situation is none other than MYEONG Seong-gi's wife, LEE Gi-ja, who is also an attorney. MYEONG Seong-gi and LEE Gi-ja's relationship is normally characterized more by conflict and competition than marital bliss, and while they prepare for an all-out collision over the neglected wife case, LEE Gyeong-ja and

CHU Hyeong-do are having their own conflict about making their private life into a public issue.

Public Enemy (2001)

Veteran homicide detective GANG Cheol-jung is a troubled man with suspicious characteristics. He is faced with an intense investigation by internal affairs following a drug investigation. In the middle of all of this, an old married couple is discovered brutally slain, and GANG, with highly tuned instincts and intuition, fingers as the suspect a suspicious man he witnessed while on stakeout, JO Gyu-hwan. But when they investigate JO, they find that he is a successful and upstanding fund manager with no criminal record. Nobody is sure whether to believe what GANG says, while bizarre murders pile up around JO Gyu-hwan. Contrary to his outward appearance, JO is a man of absolute evil, indiscriminately murdering people he doesn't like. GANG tenaciously trails JO before finally succeeding at arresting him after a fierce battle.

Silmido (2003)

Found guilty by association due to his father, who crossed over in North Korea, GANG In-chan is unable to do anything and ends up working as a thug before getting imprisoned for attempted murder. Despite its being only an attempt, he is sentenced to death, but before the sentence can be carried out he is taken by

someone to Silmido, an isolated island off the coast of Incheon. There, he finds a bunch of rough-looking men, including Sang-pil, Chang-seok, Won-hui and Geun-jae. In total, 31 men come together, forcibly isolated from society on the far-off Western island in 1968, and warrant officer KIM Jae-hyeon appears before them, telling them that it is their mission to infiltrate the palace of Kim Il-sung in North Korea and bring back his head. The 31 trainees, including In-chan, feel that, as they were going to face death anyway, this endeavor gives them the chance for a new life, and they begin hellish training under Sergeant JO, so harsh that death almost seems preferable. The formation of this special unit, called the 684 Presidential Palace Demolition Squad, has resulted from an attempt on the life of South Korean President PARK Chung-hee in a secret attack on the Blue House around that time by an armed North Korean spy named KIM Sin-jo. Following the old law of an eye for an eye and a tooth for a tooth, the government has created this special force to assassinate North Korean head of state KIM Il-sung, but in consideration of the domestic and international political environment, they ultimately decide to eliminate the trainees, including GANG In-chan. Learning of this plan, the team sneaks off of Silmido, seizes a bus and heads for the Blue House, and in the process comes to meet a tragic end.

Another Public Enemy (2004)

GANG Cheol-jung, the highest ranked prosecutor in the Public Prosecutor's Office, is a troublemaker and a hot-tempered man who doesn't hesitate to use his gun when he needs to. One day, he takes over an incident at the Myeongseon Foundation, and instinctively sensing a vicious crime, he latches tenaciously onto HAN Sang-woo, the newly appointed chairman. HAN took over the position when his brother, who was supposed to inherit the foundation, died in a suspicious accident. GANG goes through the crisis of a junior investigator losing his life, but ultimately succeeds at bringing HAN's nefarious deeds to light.

Hanbando (2005)

North and South Korea make a promise for peaceful reunification, and as the first symbol of this, they restore the discontinued Gyeongui Railroad and hold a

ceremony to mark its opening. Japan, feeling uneasy about reunification of the Korean Peninsula, claims that this railroad actually belongs to them. As proof, they say that there is contract bearing the seal of Emperor Gojong from the time of the 1907 annexation of Korea by Japan. When the two Koreas ignore this and pursue the opening of the railway line according to their schedule, Japan begins to hold armed protests, deploying a self-defense force to the East Sea. With a military clash imminent, Korean history scholar CHOE Min-jae claims that the imperial seal used by Gojong at the time of the annexation treaty was a forgery, and that the real seal is hidden in another place. The President determines that Japan's claims can be ignored if the real seal is found, and he secretly directs CHOE to unearth it. But when the Prime Minister discovers about the President's secret orders, he decides that Korean-Japanese diplomatic relations are more important for the national good and plots to neutralize CHOE's operation.

Public Enemy Returns (2008)

Disgusted by life in the homicide division, troublemaker detective GANG Cheol-jung disregards his chief's orders and skips out on the job regularly, plotting to quit as a detective. But while this is happening, a murder takes place at a high school, and GANG intuitively concludes that it is involved with organized crime. He meets with three friends who hung out with the murdered student and begins to look for clues, before ultimately uncovering that the person behind it is LEE Won-sul, the

chairman of the Geoseong Group, a phantom company put together by the mob. Feeling threatened by the tenacious pursuit of Detective GANG, LEE finally decides to leave the country by boat from Incheon. GANG chases him down to the end and, after a fierce all-out battle, succeeds in taking him down.

Filmography

Filmography

Sweet Brides (Dalkomhan Sinbu)

1988 / 95min / 35mm / 1.85:1 / Color / Mono
Production Company: Namdong Entertainment
Screenplay: KIM Sung-hong
Cinematography: SIN Ok-hyeon
Lighting: PARK Hyeon-won
Music: JEONG Su-yeon
Editing: KIM Hyeon
Starring: CHOE Jae-seong (Go-saeng), CHOE Su-ji (Yeong-ju), JEONG Jong-jun (Jae-su), PARK Hyeon-suk (Chu-ja)
Print Source: Korean Film Archive
International Sales: CJ Entertainment Inc.

Happiness Isn't Class Rankings, You Know
(Haengbogeun Seongjeok Suni Anijanayo)

1989 / 103min / 35mm / 1.85:1 / Color / Mono
Production Company: HWANG Ki-seong Productions
Screenplay: KIM Sung-hong
Cinematography: JEONG Gwang-seok
Lighting: GANG Sang-yong
Music: KIM Chang-wan
Editing: KIM Hyeon
Starring: LEE Mi-youn (LEE Eun-ju), KIM Bo-sung (KIM Bong-gu), CHOE Su-hun (AN Cheon-jae), LEE Deok-hwa (PARK Gil-ho), CHOE Su-ji (Mrs. GANG)
Print Source: Korean Film Archive
International Sales: CJ Entertainment Inc.

I Stand Up Every Day (Naneun Nal Mada Ireoseonda)

1990 / 110min / 35mm / 1.85:1 / Color / Mono
Production Company: HWANG Ki-seong Productions
Screenplay: LEE Jung-gook, KIM Sung-hong
Cinematography: JEONG Gwang-seok
Lighting: GANG Sang-yong
Music: KIM Chang-wan
Editing: KIM Hyeon
Starring: LEE Deok-hwa (JANG Baek-su), BAE Jong-ok (Eun-sil), PARK In-hwan (Mr. YUK), CHOE Ju-bong (Mr. JEONG)
Print Source: Korean Film Archive
International Sales: CJ Entertainment Inc.

Teenage Love Song
(Yeorahop Jeolmang Kkeute Bureuneun Hanaui Sarang Norae)

1991 / 89min / 35mm / 1.85:1 / Color / Mono
Production Company: Sungil Cine Art
Screenplay: JEONG Do-sang
Cinematography: YU Yeong-gil
Lighting: KIM Dong-ho
Music: GANG In-gu
Editing: KIM Hyeon
Starring: KIM Bo-sung (Jun-seok), GANG Su-ji (Chae-ok), CHOE Jin-yeong (Hyeong-su), AHN Sung-ki (Je-cheol)
International Sales: CJ Entertainment Inc.

Who Saw the Dragon's Claws? **(Nuga Yongui Baltobeul Boatneunga?)**

1991 / 98min / 35mm / 1.85:1 / Color / Mono
Production Company: Seoul Films, Inc.
Screenplay: KANG Je-kyu, NA Hong-gyun
Cinematography: JEONG Gwang-seok
Lighting: SIN Hak-seong
Music: GANG In-gu
Editing: KIM Hyeon
Starring: AHN Sung-ki (CHOE Jong-su), DOKGO Yeong-jae (KIM Hyeon-su), KIM Seong-ryeong (KIM Ji-won), SHIN Sung-il (Ruling Party Candidate), PARK Geun-hyeong (Opposition Party Candidate)
Print Source: Korean Film Archive
International Sales: CJ Entertainment Inc.

I Only Want to Live to 20 *(Seumusalkkajiman Salgo Sipeoyo)*

1992 / 103min / 35mm / 1.85:1 / Color / Mono
Production Company: Samho Films, Inc.
Screenplay: KANG Woo-suk, KIM Sang-jin
Cinematography: YU Yeong-gil
Lighting: KIM Dong-ho
Music: KIM Chang-wan
Editing: KIM Hyeon
Starring: MOON Sung-keun (CHOE Hyeong-jun), YUN Yeon-gyeong (MIN Cho-hui), CHOE Jin-yeong (KIM Cheol-su)
International Sales: CJ Entertainment Inc.

Mister Mama

1992 / 102min / 35mm / 1.85:1 / Color / Stereo
Production Company: ShinCine
Screenplay: KIM Hyeong-jun
Cinematography: SIN Ok-hyeon
Lighting: IM Jae-yeong
Music: SONG Byeong-jun
Editing: KIM Hyeon
Starring: CHOI Min-soo (Hyeong-jun), CHOI Jin-sil (Yeong-ju), KIM Il-woo (Section Chief LEE), KIM Se-jun (Hae-seok)
Print Source: Korean Film Archive
International Sales: CJ Entertainment Inc.

Two Cops

1993 / 110min / 35mm / 1.85:1 / Color / Dolby SR, Stereo
Production Company: KANG Woo-suk Productions
Screenplay: KIM Sung-hong
Cinematography: JEONG Gwang-seok
Lighting: SIN Hak-seong
Music: CHOE Gyeong-sik
Editing: KIM Hyeon
Starring: AHN Sung-ki (Detective JO), PARK Joong-hoon (Detective GANG), JI Soo-won (Su-won), SIM Yang-hong (Police Chief), YANG Taek-jo (Department Chief), YUN Mun-sik (Mr. PARK)
Print Source: Korean Film Archive
International Sales: CJ Entertainment Inc.

Killing My Wife (Manura Jugigi)

1994 / 101min / 35mm / 1.85:1 / Color / Dolby, SRD, Mono, Stereo
Production Company: KANG Woo-suk Productions
Screenplay: O Si-uk, KIM Sang-jin
Cinematography: JEONG Gwang-seok
Lighting: SIN Hak-seong
Music: CHOE Gyeong-sik
Editing: KIM Hyeon
Starring: PARK Joong-hoon (PARK Bong-su), CHOI Jin-sil (JANG So-yeong), UHM Jung-hwa (KIM Hye-ri), CHOI Jong-won (Killer), JO Hyeong-gi (Director), KWON Yong-un (Deserter)
Print Source: Korean Film Archive
International Sales: CJ Entertainment Inc.

Two Cops 2

1996 / 117min / 35mm / 1.85:1 / Color / Dolby SR
Production Company: Cinema Service, Inc.
Screenplay: KIM Sung-hong
Cinematography: SIN Ok-hyeon
Lighting: IM Jae-yeong
Music: CHOE Gyeong-sik
Editing: KIM Hyeon
Starring: PARK Joong-hoon (Detective GANG), KIM Bo-sung (Detective LEE), YANG Taek-jo (Police Chief), KIM Il-woo (Department Chief), KWON Yong-un (Kkoltong), KANG Sung-jin (Chok-sae)
Print Source: Korean Film Archive
International Sales: CJ Entertainment Inc.

Bedroom and Courtroom (Saenggwabu Wijaryo Cheonggu Sosong)

1998 / 116min / 35mm / 1.85:1 / Color / SRD
Production Company: Cinema Service, Inc.
Screenplay: O Si-uk
Cinematography: JEONG Gwang-seok
Lighting: KIM Dong-ho
Music: KIM Dong-seong
Editing: KIM Hyeon
Starring: AHN Sung-ki (MYEONG Seong-gi), MOON Sung-keun (CHU Hyeong-do), HWANG Cine (LEE Gyeong-ja), SHIM Hye-jin (LEE Gi-ja), MYEONG Gye-nam (JO Se-chang)
Print Source: Korean Film Archive
International Sales: CJ Entertainment Inc.

Public Enemy (Gonggongui Jeok)

2001 / 135min / 35mm / 1.85:1 / Color / Dolby SR
Production Company: Cinema Service, Inc.
Screenplay: BAEK Seung-jae, JEONG Yun-seop, KIM Hyeong-jeong, CHAE Yun-seok
Cinematography: KIM Seong-bok
Lighting: SIN Hak-seong
Art Direction: BAE Mu-cheol
Music: JO Yeong-uk
Editing: GO Im-pyo
Starring: SUL Kyoung-gu (GANG Cheol-jung), LEE Sung-jae (JO Gyu-hwan), KANG Shin-il (Chief EOM), LEE Mun-sik (San-su), SUNG Ji-ru (Dae-gil), YU Hae-jin (Yong-man)
Print Source: Korean Film Archive
International Sales: CJ Entertainment Inc.

Silmido

2003 / 135min / 35mm / 2.35:1 / Color / SRD
Production Company: Hanmaek Pictures, Inc.; Plenus Cinema Service, Inc.
Screenplay: KIM Hui-jae
Cinematography: KIM Seong-bok
Lighting: SIN Hak-seong
Music: JO Yeong-uk
Editing: GO Im-pyo
Starring: SUL Kyoung-gu (In-chan), AHN Sung-ki (Jae-hyeon), HUH Joon-ho (Sergeant JO), LIM Won-hee (Won-hee), JUNG Jae-young (Sang-pil), KANG Sung-jin (Chan-seok), KANG Shin-il (Geun-jae)
Print Source: Korean Film Archive
International Sales: CJ Entertainment Inc.

Another Public Enemy (Gonggongui Jeok 2)

2005 / 148min / 35mm / 2.35:1 / Color / Dolby SRD
Production Company: Cinema Service, Inc.
Screenplay: KIM Hui-jae
Cinematography: KIM Seong-bok
Lighting: SIN Hak-seong
Art Direction: LEE Yo-han
Music: HAN Jae-gwon
Editing: GO Im-pyo
Starring: SUL Kyoung-gu (GANG Cheol-jung), JEOUNG Jun-ho (HAN Sang-ho), KANG Shin-il (KIM Shin-il), PARK Geun-hyeong (Vice President), BYUN Hee-bong (AN Hyo-jun)
Print Source: Korean Film Archive
International Sales: CJ Entertainment Inc.

Hanbando

2006 / 147min / 35mm / 2.35:1 / Color / Dolby SRD
Production Company: KnJ Entertainment
Screenplay: KIM Hui-jae, LEE Hyo-cheol
Cinematography: CHOE Yeong-taek
Art Direction: LEE Tae-hun
Music: HAN Jae-gwon
Editing: GO Im-pyo
Starring: AHN Sung-ki (President), MOON Sung-keun (Prime Minister), CHO Jae-hyun (CHOE Min-jae), CHA In-pyo (LEE Sang-hyeon), KANG Shin-il (KIM Yu-sik), KIM Sang-joong (Emperor Gojong), KANG Soo-yeon (Empress Min)
Print Source: Korean Film Archive
International Sales: CJ Entertainment Inc.

Public Enemy Returns (Gang Cheol-jung: Gonggongui Jeok 1-1)

2008 / 125min / 35mm / 2.35:1 / Color / Dolby SRD
Production Company: KnJ Entertainment
Screenplay: JANG Jin
Cinematography: KIM Seong-bok
Lighting: SIN Hak-seong
Art Direction: O Seon-ho
Music: JO Yeong-uk
Editing: GO Im-pyo
Starring: SUL Kyoung-gu (GANG Cheol-jung), JUNG Jae-young (LEE Won-sul), KANG Shin-il (Chief EOM), YU Hae-jin (Yong-man), LEE Mun-sik (San-su)
Print Source: Korean Film Archive
International Sales: CJ Entertainment Inc.

About the Author

OH Dong-jin

OH Dong-jin worked as a film reporter for the Munhwa Ilbo, Yonhap News and YTN before serving as chief of the news research office and a member of the editing committee for the film weekly *FILM 2.0*, chief editor for the film weekly *Cineverse* and director of the content production bureau for the Internet film magazine *nKINO*. He is currently an invited professor in the film department at Dong-Eui University, a member of the film specialists' committee at PRESSian, a member of the executive committee for the Busan International Film Festival, chief director of the broadcasting production company D&D Media, and a member of the planning committee for the art theater Kring Cinema.

He has hosted the programs *Cinema Heaven* on EBS TV and *Cine 24* on YTN, and he is current appearing on the specialists' panel for the KNN program *Cineport*.

Index